ROXANNE HOBBS is a key influenc
and Diversity agenda in the adver
The Hobbs Consultancy as a result
the advertising industry could and sh

a much greater degree. She soon realised that solely coaching women advocated the message that women are "broken" and "need fixing", a far cry from the reality. Roxanne also noticed that there are many other groups that also lack the necessary confidence to assert themselves in the advertising industry. She broadened the scope of her work accordingly, with a particularly interest in introverts.

In March 2017, Roxanne's eldest son was diagnosed with ASD. She was immediately struck by how we ask those that aren't neurotypical to change so that they conform with neurotypical norms. She is now heavily involved in sparking and consequently sustaining a conversation about Neurodiversity in the advertising industry – so that individuals with potential are equipped with the necessary skills and knowledge to thrive in this environment.

Roxanne uses the Co-Active model in her coaching, which is built on the cornerstone that we are all innately resourceful, creative and whole. Roxanne is also a certified Daring Way™ Facilitator – using Brené Brown's curriculum to support participants in showing up and being seen in the workplace.

She lives in Hackney with her husband, two sons and a crazy puggle.

DIVERTED

Roxanne Hobbs

SilverWood

Published in 2018 by SilverWood Books

SilverWood Books Ltd
14 Small Street, Bristol, BS1 1DE, United Kingdom
www.silverwoodbooks.co.uk

ISBN 978-1-78132-758-6 (paperback)
ISBN 978-1-78132-759-3 (ebook)

British Library Cataloguing in Publication Data
A CIP catalogue record for this book is available from the British Library

Page design and typesetting by SilverWood Books
Printed on responsibly sourced paper

Courage is forged in pain, but not in all pain. Pain that is denied or ignored becomes fear or hate.[1]

1   Brené Brown (2017) *Braving the Wilderness : The Quest for True Belonging and the Courage to Stand Alone*

Contents

Introduction

I was beside myself and furious. Finn was hurt and very, very upset. I needed to get Leo out of the room and upstairs to his bedroom. Right now. But he was a large five-year-old and I realised I couldn't lift him anymore. He started fighting back and the situation escalated further. We battled it out up to his bedroom. It was not my finest hour as a parent. Pure fury. At him and myself. I shut the door and sat in his bedroom blocking the door so he couldn't leave. Finn was still crying downstairs. All I could think was, "We need to be able to feel safe in our house. Leo is making me feel unsafe". I took some deep breaths so I at least looked calm on the outside. We were staying there until everyone had calmed down.

Leo then lost it. He kicked, bit and hit me like I have never experienced before. I was at a total loss as to what to do. I wasn't going to fight back, clearly, but I couldn't let him do this to me. Again, the thought came up, "We need to be able to feel safe in our house". It was a turning point. As I waited for the calm to descend, and my own breathing and heart rate to slow, I knew we couldn't wait any longer for our Autism Spectrum Disorder assessment. The 'not knowing' made situations like this even more impossible. The very next morning I called up Hackney Ark (the home of

Special Educational Needs provision in the borough of Hackney where we live) in desperation. They offered us an assessment the very next week.

I couldn't believe this is where we were. That my son was being tested for autism. That I was the parent of somebody with additional needs. This wasn't the path that I had planned for us to take.

I have learnt so much about what resilience is, and equally what it isn't, in the past year. I am fortunate enough to work as a coach and consultant in the diversity and inclusivity arena, and regularly give talks about resilience and supporting people to show up as themselves. Yet this year has accelerated my understanding. We learn so much when we find ourselves in the dark and have a good look around there.

My son Leo has always been one of my most persistent and effective teachers. I remember trying to wean him – it would take him half an hour to eat a piece of toast. I'd be sat there, impatient and yet marvelling at what he was teaching me about patience. Leo is now in the autumn term of Year One and has taught me more than I could have imagined this past year – *about myself.* It is certainly true that the times in our lives in which we face our most challenging struggles are those that are the most ripe for learning and wisdom. I wouldn't wish the past year of our lives on anyone. And I do know that we have the most fantastic son, who I wouldn't swap for the world, and that I have greater self–awareness and clarity about my reason for being here than I did before.

Last October, I was called in after school to speak to Leo's class teacher. He had just started in reception a month before. She thought we needed to get 'special needs' involved in his education. I remember sitting down on those tiny chairs they have in early years classrooms and the teacher asking me what I'd noticed about Leo and what others had noticed. She kept asking questions until

I mentioned casually that a yoga teacher had once said to me she thought he might have autism.

And then she jumped in.

"That's our concern too – we want to arrange a meeting to discuss him with the SENCO." (SENCO is the special educational needs co-ordinator.) Since then we've been through an assessment, a diagnosis of high functioning autism and, quite frankly, a hugely challenging year.

It's worth pointing out here that those with 'high functioning autism' appear to cope better with the outside world than those who are described as being 'low functioning' (and both are terms that the autism community rally against). Leo was slightly late to start speaking aged two and clearly has sufficient autistic characteristics to warrant a diagnosis. I am well aware that there are other parents out there struggling with much more difficult behaviours, a fact that has become painfully clear to my husband and me since becoming reluctant members of the autism community in Hackney, our corner of London. Also, even though I have a lot of 'tools' that I can use to support my resilience (learnt in my coaching training), I have often wondered how those who haven't spent five years focusing on such topics manage to get through it.

Even so, when it comes to you and your own life, it doesn't always mean that you can pick yourselves straight back up again and adapt to your newfound circumstances. Everything that I have learnt as a coach has been incredibly useful, and yet I have also needed further support. And that's OK. As someone who speaks publically about resilience, there's certainly no point in beating myself up about suddenly finding myself feeling less than resilient (although that is a thought that I have had).

I also want to offer what support I can to other parents who find themselves in this situation. I found there was very little in the way of literature that focused on supporting the parent. If you google 'coping as a mum with autism' you invariably get results about mums who have autism themselves, which is a whole different challenge. In his introduction to the wonderful *Fall Down 7 Times, Get Up 8*[2], David Mitchell reviews the literature available and says that self-confessional memoirs by parents provide little in the way of practical support. I disagree, and also aim to offer more. Understanding what other parents are going through is *invaluable* at a time when you feel so alone and that it is only you that is going through such difficulty. I set out to share authentically our struggle and yet also to pepper that with research about resilience – to provide support for anyone adapting to change.

It is important as a parent to up your understanding of the change to which you are adapting. And I sense that a lot of us do this while neglecting to take care of ourselves. It's a well-known trait of mothers, autism in the family or not, to put the needs of others first, and themselves last. I'm not sure how much support you can give your child when you are feeling all at sea, and struggling to accept the situation in which you find yourself. It is totally normal and acceptable to find this situation challenging and a struggle, and my hope is that by sharing my experience I can offer parents going through this difficult transition some learnings through which they can focus on themselves as well as their child. And also, to know that they are not alone.

Finally, and I hesitate to write this because of the boldness of the statement, I would like to raise the bar, just a tiny bit, on how we understand and relate to those with autism. According to the National Autistic Society[3], around 700,000 people in the UK are on the autism spectrum (so, more than one in 100 people) meaning

2   Higashida, Naoki (2017) *Fall Down 7 Times Get Up 8: A Young Man's Voice from the Silence of Autism* with an introduction by David Mitchell

3   http://www.autism.org.uk

that, together with their families, autism is a part of daily life for 2.8 million people. They define autism as a "lifelong developmental disability that affects how people perceive the world and interact with others". There is no cure – if you have an autistic brain, you will have an autistic brain for life. It is also a spectrum condition meaning that although all those with autism share certain difficulties, their autism affects them in profoundly different ways. And that there is a huge range of struggle contained within this spectrum. People with autistic brains often say they feel overwhelmed by the world and that this causes them considerable anxiety. The most common struggle is in connecting with others – understanding and relating to other people can be harder for people with autism. As I've sought to understand my own resilience more, I have come to a greater understanding of how we all struggle, including those with autism, and have really been surprised by the commonality of much of our struggle.

My professional purpose is to champion inclusivity. I run workshops and give talks about how we can encourage, especially in the workplace, people to show up as themselves and to be valued for doing just that. Much of my early resistance to intervention was based on the thought that it wasn't encouraging the person with autism to be themselves – it was teaching them how to fit in with what the rest of society expects as 'normal'. It is similar to the paradox facing parents of boys that Rebecca Asher outlines in *Man Up*[4]. We want our boys to be themselves (and resist conforming to detrimental versions of masculinity such as 'real men don't cry'), and yet it is also true that they will benefit from understanding the 'rules' of society and its expectations of them as boys and men.

Sometimes autism is a devastating developmental condition and a lifelong disability. It is also a naturally occurring form of

4   Asher, Rebecca (2016) *Man Up: Boys, Men and Breaking the Male Rules*

cognitive difference, sometimes (but not always) related to certain forms of genius[5]. Often, I think it is our fear of difference and the unhelpful stereotypes around autism that creates many of the difficulties for those with autism (with the huge caveat that it is indeed sometimes a devastating developmental disability too). I call upon the experts and researchers to up their game in understanding autism (our understanding has moved on little since the 1960s[6]). And I think society can equally up our game in understanding this difference and co-creating a world in which we can all thrive.

5   Silberman, Steve (2015) *NeuroTribes: The Legacy of Autism and How to Think Smarter About People Who Think Differently*

6   Mitchell, David (2017) https://www.theguardian.com/society/2017/jul/08/david-mitchell-son-autism-diagnosis-advice

1

On Being Blindsided

You know that feeling you sometimes have that everything is going along just fine in your world, and you start to wonder what's around the corner? Your marriage is going ok, your kids seem to be doing well, your business is finally getting off the ground... You can't quite believe how lucky you are and, equally, can't quite relax in to the gratitude and joy of it all. Something must be around the corner...

Last October, I was completely blindsided.

What does that mean? According to the Cambridge Dictionary, "To surprise someone, usually with harmful results"[7].

I went in to pick my kids up after school with a clear idea in my head of who my children were. Equally, I felt sure about my husband, myself and our relationship. Life was treating me well. Leo's school teacher wanted a quick chat with me after school and mumbled something about "getting special needs involved" (meaning the Special Needs Co-ordinator). After an interrogation about different people's perspectives on Leo, she made the suggestion that he might be autistic. This one sentence, one suggestion, seemed to absolutely pull the rug out from underneath me. Suddenly, it

---

7   http://dictionary.cambridge.org/dictionary/english/blindside

seemed like I had to reassess everything. It was as if I'd been given a new pair of glasses to look through at the things that mattered to me most, and that I would never be able to take them off again.

Prior to that week in October, I had never had the conscious thought that Leo might have autism. I saw a lovely, kind, sweet-natured and introverted boy when I looked at him, who loved his cuddles with his Mama and who, on occasion, could be incredibly demanding. Your typical five-year-old. I struggled out in to the playground and had to ask for help. One of the mums helped me round up both Leo and Finn (who was three at the time) and get us out in to the street. I had lost the ability to communicate coherently, which became a theme of the months ahead. Somehow, I got them home. My husband, Steve, came home and I had to wait until we'd got the kids to bed to sit him down and talk him through what had happened.

After something knocks you like this, self-trust is often one of the very first casualties. I had brought up Leo alongside his father (and my husband) Steve for five years and it *had not crossed my mind* that he might have autism. How could we, his parents, not have noticed? What else might be going on underneath our noses that we were blind to? I started questioning every parenting decision we were making and became hyper vigilant to his activities. Leo gave me a hug when I was upset? Can't have autism. He started talking about the names of the gates in the park in the middle of a conversation about football. What if they're right? What else might I have missed? In what other ways might I be missing the blindingly obvious and making some terrible parenting decisions?

Our other son was struggling with soiling himself at this stage, and I hurriedly made a doctor's appointment for him. Up until now I'd trusted my instinct that he'd grow out of it, but suddenly I didn't trust my intuition and found myself reaching out for other people's opinions. This turned out to be a lengthy process in itself. The doctor noted that my youngest hadn't been putting on adequate weight and suggested that he might have coeliac disease. We went to the hospital for blood tests which, as I'm sure you can imagine, are pretty tricky to take for a three-year-old. We then stopped giving him gluten and convinced ourselves there was a slight improvement. The poor child wasn't allowed gluten for two months, including during a holiday in an all-inclusive resort with pastries galore. Sorry Finn! We returned home to be told that the hospital had lost the results and the gluten had to be reintroduced so that the bloods didn't record a false positive. There was no significant decline on introducing gluten. Finally, about three months later, we were given the all clear. Finn doesn't have coeliac disease – rather the doctor is now convinced it's something psychological. This is something I 'knew' a few months ago. I had just failed to trust my maternal instinct because my self-trust had truly deteriorated.

We were told that many cases of autism are thought to be genetic, particularly through the male line. We started scrutinising Steve's family history. We were told that the probability of having a child with autism increases with IVF conception, which we had needed to conceive Leo. Steve started looking at some of his own personality traits and saw autistic characteristics. We started questioning everything about our lives – our family, our relationships, our choices. When I'm feeling acutely stressed, I often lose the capacity for empathy. If I'm having a blazing row with my husband, I have the tendency to shut down and can stop feeling any sense of what might be going on for him – even if he is visibly upset. If I'm overloaded at work, I can get caught up in a rigid way of thinking, focusing on the task at hand and overlooking the feelings of those around me. There's a really big clue in here that I missed at the time.

It's meaningless really which side of the family it has come from. What is important is that people can lose the capacity for empathy the more anxious, stressed or overloaded they become. This isn't just an autism trait (and as I later learn, it might be more pertinent to say that this isn't even an autism trait. The difficulty in empathising might well be one of the most harmful myths about autism[8] and is explored further later in this book). It would seem to be a human trait. The National Autistic Society (NAS) is doing a lot of work educating people that autism is a result of 'too much information'. For a while, I sat with the premise that the information overload in their brain may well be behind the difficulty in empathising with others, and I also saw Leo's apparent ability to empathise as proof that he couldn't have autism.

The more I started to read and learn about autism, the more I started questioning our future too. Things weren't looking too rosy ahead. I read about problems children with autism have with anxiety and depression, of bullying, of learning disabilities and physical challenges. I learnt that back in the 1940s doctors blamed 'refrigerator mothers'[9] for children's autism, claiming it was down to a lack of maternal love, a practice that seems to have continued until the 1970s. I made it my mission to learn as much as I could about the condition and, in the process, scared the hell out of myself. At the same time, we were nearing the end of the autumn term. It was dark already by late afternoon, the kids were exhausted and there was a rigmarole of events that Leo had to attend and which I sensed he wouldn't enjoy. We were called to pick him up early from the pantomime trip because he was asking to leave. For the school nativity play, he wore bright red noise cancelling earphones as he had been complaining that it was too noisy in

8   www.scientificamerican.com/article/people-with-autism-can -read-emotions-feel-empathy1/

9   Kanner L (1949) "Problems of nosology and psychodynamics in early childhood autism", Am J Orthopsychiatry

the school hall. I was barely holding it together. It felt as though one day I had a gorgeous five-year-old, and that he had gradually been replaced by a child with autism. Leo had never been one for fixed routines, the stereotype of many children on the spectrum; rather he likes to *be in charge* when he's feeling anxious and overwhelmed. One day as we were leaving school, he started giving me ever more intricate directions for how we needed to get home and I started sobbing. *I can't do this, Leo. I'm so sorry.* We got an Uber home – Leo looked surprised but fortunately acquiesced.

Soon after this we went away for a couple of weeks to get some winter sunshine. The boys were impeccably behaved on the early morning six-hour flight, which eventually left after a three-hour delay. At the airport in Cape Verde, something had gone wrong with the paperwork and everyone needed to reapply for their visas. Hence further waiting and some very tired and fed up individuals. My kids started running around like crazy in the line, only for a policewoman to escort us to the front of the queue because she could see we were struggling with the children. An elderly guy in the queue started to kick off at us, believing us to have pushed in – "We've been waiting for hours here – there's a queue!" I tried to stay calm and point out that we had been asked by the police to move to the front of the queue. And then the dreaded line came: "Can't you control your children?" Immediately, I was in shame and so spoke to Steve about this feeling on the way to the hotel. This is a shame resilience practice that I have been trained to do in my work as a coach – the idea being that we can move through this visceral emotion faster if we speak about it to those we trust, when in reality it's usually the last thing that you want to talk about. In the taxi, we simply told each other how we felt. I told him how I feel like a terrible mother when my children are out of control, and he told me how he doesn't feel "good enough". Yet still that man's tormenting voice ran around in my head for the first few days of my holiday.

The thing is, kids can go crazy when they've got off a flight whether they have autism or not. That's certainly not a story you could only tell about a child with autism. Yet everything that was happening to us now had started to be viewed through that lens. I was berating the man at the airport, in my head, for not knowing that my son might have autism. And of course, why would he know? It's invisible. On so many occasions, I've wished there was an internationally recognised gesture to let people around me know of his condition so that all of the responsibility isn't on me to create the environment that he needs. (That same trip, the poor child was randomly selected at security to go in those new body-scanning machines at Heathrow. Inside I was panicking about whether he'd cope and wished the security team could be made aware of his autism). I realised that the shame button that man pushed wasn't about being a bad mother at all. It was about demanding or requiring special treatment. *Who are you to think we should do things differently to accommodate your family?*

Autism became the lens through which we experienced everything on that holiday. Leo wouldn't join in at football, he struggled at the kids' club and he became obsessed with measuring the depth of the swimming pool. Autistic behaviours? Conversely, he tried the water slides, made a new friend and, when Steve flew home early because of work, didn't seem impacted at all by the change. Not autistic behaviours – they've got it wrong. We realised later that the new friend was Dutch and spoke no English at all – they simply threw a ball back and forth to each other. She might even have had autism too! We also noticed how much tiredness and poor diet impacted on Leo, which was something we made a note to return to and learn more about.

Uncertainty pervaded those winter months. We felt shocked, like a rug had been pulled from under us. For a while I felt like we didn't know how to parent Leo because of the uncertainty. We decided together to do what we felt was right for him, even if sometimes that was different to how we parent Finn. And we realised that is exactly what we've always done. Leo seemed to do better at school in the spring term but things came to a head one evening after school. After school is always a tricky time when Leo is tired and some kind of altercation happens between the brothers. I learned that this is a common tricky time for children with autism – school has been overwhelming and they have been coping with that all day, and need to decompress when they get home. Leo ended up whacking Finn, who was understandably very upset. I tried to get Leo out of the room for some time out, but realised I couldn't really lift him anymore. He started fighting back and the situation soon escalated. I was beside myself and furious – with him and with myself. For some reason, all I could think was, "We need to be able to feel safe in our house. Leo is making me feel unsafe", and we battled it out up to his bedroom. It was not my finest hour as a parent. Once there, I sat calmly (on the outside at least), blocking his door, and told him we were staying there until everyone had calmed down. Leo then proceeded to totally lose it and kicked, bit and hit me like I had never experienced before. I was at a total loss as to what to do. I wasn't going to fight back, clearly, but I couldn't let him do this to me. Again, the thought came up, "We need to be able to feel safe in our house". The next day I called up Hackney Ark (the home of Special Educational Needs provision in the borough of Hackney where we live) who we were waiting to get in touch with about an assessment appointment.

Resilience, for me, is about properly adapting to changes in circumstance. Change happens and so we, as resilient beings, need to be able to adapt to that, hopefully with a sprinkle of further learning and a dash of grace. I think it's about seeing life's difficulties as learning opportunities, as then they categorically can't be seen as failures. I don't think resilience is about faking a positive attitude as you go through your darkest struggles. It is about facing the struggle, digging around in it and coming to a clearer understanding of yourself and your situation. The challenge is that, when something hard happens, we can often be so shocked, so knocked off our feet, that we lose sight of that higher-level objective and instead need to focus on just coping with what is happening in the here and now.

As well as meaning "to surprise someone, usually with harmful results"[10], a further definition of "blindside" I have seen (from Google) is "to make (someone) unable to perceive the truth of the situation". When an unexpected event like this happens, it takes us a while to wrap our heads around what is actually going on. Elisabeth Kübler-Ross's change curve, originally proposed in the 1960s[11] in relation to dealing with death, has been widely used as a method of helping people react to significant change or upheaval. Her book *On Death and Dying* introduces the now famous idea of the five stages of dealing with death, which are widely used as a means of coping with any major upheaval. The first stage is denial and isolation, followed by anger, bargaining, depression and acceptance.

It's worth saying that Steve didn't go through such a shock and heightened experience at the beginning of this process. At the time, I made up that he wasn't processing what was happening and that it was going to hit him at some stage. When I asked him about it further down the line, he told me that it was because, for him, Asperger's Syndrome was a positive label, and that was the language that the school used when we subsequently went in together to

10   http://dictionary.cambridge.org/dictionary/english/blindside

11   Kübler-Ross (1969) *On Death and Dying*

speak to them. (Asperger's Syndrome is not a formal diagnosis that is given any longer as it has been 'folded in' to the diagnosis of High Functioning Autism). Steve told me, "At the time, I thought Asperger's was something quite different to what people think of as autism. It also didn't particularly surprise me – when Leo was younger, and we went to the play park together, I thought it was unusual that he'd stand by the fence and watch the buses go past, rather than playing with the other kids and the equipment there. I was happy to see Leo as special and a bit different."

It is possible that the initial language used (for Steve it was Asperger's, whereas for me it was Autism), and our understanding of these terms, had an impact on our initial reaction. However, more pertinently, I think the roots of our relative ease and distress were in what this meant for our relationship and connection with Leo. Steve felt closer to his son. "I've struggled to be understood my whole life. People don't really get me and, in my latter career history, I have been passed over for new opportunities because I'm a bit different, while I feel I am more than capable. If anything, these conversations helped me to see a bit of Leo in me, and I found it easy to focus on the things that Leo does really well – reading, numbers, focus, systematic understanding..." The opposite was happening for me. I had already noticed, when both the SENCO and a colleague pointed it out, how far away these characteristics were from my personal world view and approach.

I had spent the past five years of my life learning about and teaching empathy. I actively champion vulnerability and in the blurb for my business talk about how the most important things *can't* be measured quantitatively (such as trust, empathy and inclusion). What if I was wrong to hold all of these things as important? What if this was going to move me further away from connecting with my son? (I'm not sure if it's a deep lack of confidence in my own approach, or a vastly overdeveloped empathic perspective, to go straight to a belief in my five-year old son's world view as more salient over my own). Either way, Steve felt closer to Leo from the start of these conversations, whereas I felt further away, more alienated and less understood.

Denial was clearly a key feature of this initial phase for me. This was complicated to work through as I did have genuine reservations about whether Leo had autism or not. Other parents seemed as surprised by the suggestion as I was. For a while, I was convinced the school was being overzealous in their approach. Perhaps that they'd just been on an 'Autism Awareness' course and were seeking to implement their findings? It is obvious, looking back now, that I was in denial. The questioning, the hyper vigilance, the confusion about my own intuitive voice – all point to shock and denial. However, I know that at the time I would have railed against (and did indeed rail against) people pointing this out to me. I felt it was my duty as a parent to ensure that Leo got an accurate and fair diagnosis and so I did challenge and question throughout.

I was hyper vigilant to any kind of mixed messages I received from the school. I went to see the Special Needs Co-ordinator to ask, "Are you sure?" She was. But before I accepted that and left, I made her go through all of the other potential special needs that children have – just to check that it wasn't perhaps something else that was affecting Leo. I went to the head of the lower juniors to complain I was getting mixed messages from the class teacher, who one minute was telling me Leo was doing fantastically and the next was telling me he was incapable of doing his shoes up properly and needed to be taught. (Struggles with fine motor skills are a characteristic of the autism spectrum and this teacher could perhaps have given him some leeway given her suspicions about him at this stage.) Really this was all because I was in denial, but it was exceedingly difficult to name it as that when I was in it.

During that time I was mistaking my denial for "questioning the validity of the statements made about Leo", the one thing I wasn't in denial about was the huge impact all of this was having on me. I got clear on my feelings pretty quickly and allowed myself time to sit with them and examine them. Many people, when something hard happens, pretend that it isn't happening and push their emotions down. Some people use drink to numb, others push their emotions down until they are unleashed in a fit of rage, and others push it down until their emotions display themselves as physical symptoms[12]. We don't live in a culture where it is considered the done thing to sit and examine the pain – much better to find a way to get rid of the hurt as soon as possible. I confess, sometimes it felt like there wasn't enough wine in the world to take the pain away. At other times, I managed to dig deep and sit with the painful feelings that came up. This book really is a testament to that. A great practice is to start naming these emotions to be sure that you are being present to them and I was clear from the start that the pain was something to do with shock, grief and shame.

It is normal, in a reaction to change, to temporarily slow down and become 'less capable'. For someone who was (is) used to being fairly high achieving and very 'on top' of things, to suddenly find myself incapable of organising simple things, such as our family meals, was infuriating. There was a fog that I couldn't lift. Looking at it practically, I imagine that my brainpower was being used to try and make sense of the situation with Leo, leaving little left to cope with everyday life.

Of course, Leo was carrying on as normal during this time period. He didn't have any idea what was going on. Or perhaps he did as, on reflection, his behaviour was far worse than any time

12 Brown, Brené (2016) *Rising Strong*

previously and any time since. Perhaps he was somehow intuitively picking up on the change in atmosphere and confusion in the household. Change, of course, is a well-known struggle for those with autism. In *NeuroTribes*[13], Steve Silberman talks of 'The Wizard of Clapham Common', Henry Cavendish – a prominent scientist in the late 1700s who, today, is best known for his discovery of hydrogen. Through a modern lens, his autistic tendencies become apparent. Silberman tells of Cavendish's evening walks and how "his route, like his departure time, never varied". He so valued consistency, or so disagreed with change, that "he had made only one revision to this itinerary in a quarter of a century". A more recent example in the same book is 'The Boy Who Loves Green Straws'. A young boy called Leo (I discover there are a lot of Leos in the autism literature[14]) insists on watching Hayao Miyazaki's enchanting animated tale *My Neighbour Totoro* every evening. He has watched it with his father, on a nightly basis, literally thousands of times.

These examples are extreme (of humanity, perhaps not of autism). Equally, I do think we all struggle with change. Change, especially when unexpected, can give rise to feelings of stress, anxiety and being overwhelmed. A week away can feel incredibly restorative. The return to the 'real world' can take some adapting to. Our struggle with change is perhaps why Kübler-Ross's change curve so caught the public imagination – it showed people that it is possible to move through change, and that our struggles with it are incredibly normal. Drawing a parallel with what is going on for Leo, I think much of his brainpower is used up trying to cope with the constant state of change that is everyday life, that he perhaps struggles with some of the societal niceties that are expected of

13 Silberman, Steve (2015) *NeuroTribes: The Legacy of Autism and the Future of Neurodiversity*

14 Another Leo is Leo Kanner – an Austrian psychiatrist and social activist best known for his work related to autism, and unfortunately the key thinker behind the 'refrigerator mothers' theory. We'll talk more about him later…

him. An understandable response to that would be to impose some kind of order on what he is able to control.

And though I didn't know what the future would hold, I did know, sitting on the floor of Leo's room, that I was feeling a huge loss – initially the loss of certainty in my world and loss of trust in the professionals around me that felt like grief – and that there was some kind of shame present for me. I was also aware I needed to get closer practically to the truth of the situation. I needed clarity about Leo's diagnosis and also clarity about my own emotional field and what sat behind these overwhelming and painful emotions. I couldn't do this alone. We needed help. We had been on the waiting list for an assessment appointment for three months by this stage. After my desperate phone all, Hackney Ark rang me back saying that they'd had a cancellation and we could go in the next week for Leo's assessment.

Supporting yourself through the initial shock when your life is diverted.

1   Hyper vigilance and denial are to be expected when your life shifts direction. Go easy on yourself and, if you can, embrace activities that slow your speeding brain down. It may feel as though you need to spend all of your energy working through this sudden diversion, yet time spent looking after yourself is also a worthwhile investment. It can feel like the last thing in the world you want to do, but going swimming, to yoga, out for a short walk in the sunshine or to a local café for tea and cake, might give you the resources and energy to keep going.

2   You will not feel like this forever. Just like the bone-crushing tiredness of having a newborn, this period in which your

brain struggles to make sense of your reality is truly a stage. You will feel differently as time progresses, even if you have the same challenges to deal with. Remind yourself of adjustments you have made in the past and how you have come through the other side.

3 Be mindful of what literature you read. The internet is truly a scary place and, because of confirmation bias (the tendency of the mind to look for information that confirms your current world view), you will be drawn to articles that reflect your scared state of mind. There are positive and life-affirming works out there (I loved the novel *The Rosie Project*[15] and the non-fictional *NeuroTribes*[16]), and helpful organisations (the National Autistic Society[17] have a helpline). There is also a lot of scaremongering and quasi science.

15   Simsion, Graeme (2013) *The Rosie Project*

16   Silberman, Steve (2015) *NeuroTribes : The Legacy of Autism and the Future of Neurodiversity*

17   http://www.autism.org.uk

2

Struggling To Trust

Trust, or rather lack of trust, was a key theme in those first few months. My relationship with the school remained on patchy ground. They seemed unclear who had called the parent – teacher meetings we go in for, even though they had asked us to book the appointments in. I found it hard to trust that the school would know more about our son than I or my husband did. We held a meeting to talk about the upcoming assessment and, for a while, it was thought that Hackney Ark would send someone in to the school to observe Leo in his classroom. Strangely, the SENCO asked that the form teacher get out all of the 'interventions' that they had been using, and had since stopped using, "as it will save time". I found myself doubting the school's intentions. It seemed like they were after a diagnosis from the assessment, whereas we want a true assessment.

I found myself at odds with his class teacher. I had struggled with her since the beginning of the year when she had told me that my son was quiet and, "not to worry, I'll bash it out of him by the end of the year". Being a fervent supporter of the right of the introvert to be quiet, I had been furious – and yet found myself clamming up. Equally, after his first school-based swimming lesson, when she had told me that I had better teach my son to get dressed as he "didn't have a clue what he was doing after swimming", I had left the school in tears and unable to find my voice. We had been working with Leo on getting himself dressed for months and I discovered that this is something that kids on the spectrum do struggle with. Every morning there was a standoff. We were trying to let him go at his own pace but ended up pushing him beyond what he was ready for, partly because the school was pushing us and partly because I felt like I was failing at this basic parenting duty.

My trust in myself almost disappeared. I started questioning my ability to parent and couldn't understand why I'd had this enormous blind spot. I wondered if the work I did had got in the way. I do a lot of work with future female leaders – and so am pretty knowledgeable about introversion and also inclusion in the workplace. I preach that people should be able to show up as themselves and be valued for it. In fact, inclusion is one of my core three values (alongside courage and authenticity). When I look at Leo, I see an introvert who is interested in the facts and data of the world around him. And yet, here I was being told that my son's 'being himself' was somehow a disability or a disorder. He needed to adapt so as to fit in. At first my experience of all of the interventions were requests for him to shift how he turned up, rather than a world that would just let him be himself. I struggled for a long time with the label 'autistic' as it implies a disorder where I see personality. I still do, to be honest.

I struggled at work. I do one to one coaching sessions and found my concentration disappearing in my sessions. I made mistakes and lost the thread of the stories my clients were telling me. In one session, I used the wrong name for my client's boss and berated myself for hours afterwards that I wasn't strong enough to be able to support my clients. My supervisor told me about a saying she had come across – that the success of the intervention depends on the inner condition of the intervener[18]. She meant that if I, as the intervener, wasn't doing well, there wasn't too much hope of my coaching interventions having a positive impact. I was on the floor and trying to pick myself up every day to support other women with their career challenges. I apologise to all of the clients I saw during that time period. I really wasn't operating at my best.

The day before Leo's assessment, I had managed to secure a therapy appointment for myself. I really needed somewhere to vent and to explore some of my feelings on the topic. Someone had recommended a therapist who was, at that time, still away in New Zealand and so we needed to conduct the session over Skype. I sat on my bed upstairs and started to tell her about the situation in which I found myself. As soon as I said that Leo was being assessed for autism on the request of the school and I had doubts about whether he had autism, she jumped in. "If you don't think he's autistic, then he isn't." Hmmm. What is going on in my family then? We spoke some more, including about my husband's struggles and how he uses running to help regulate his emotions. "The only problem in your house is that your husband is an addict". Wow. Blow to the stomach – and yet I inconceivably stayed quiet. I told her that my husband is setting up a running business. "Good luck with that," she said sarcastically. You would have thought I'd have told her where to go, and to have got off the phone. But I had no trust in myself at this stage. I sat there, being told by another so-called expert, what was going on in my family and I completely lost my voice. I came off the phone blindsided a second time.

Needless to say, none of the adults in our house got much sleep that night. And this was the night before Leo's assessment.

---

18   This quote seems to be attributable to Bill O'Brien, the late CEO of Hanover Insurance; https://www.presencing.com/theoryu

I didn't give Steve the full details of what had happened on the Skype session, but he could see I was knocked by it. I told him that the therapist had suggested the family dynamic was probably impacting upon Leo. I shudder now when I think what he went through that evening, as even that limited information was devastating for him. He got up early in the morning and went for a run, which compounded my confusion. *Is he addicted to running?* I know he runs to numb the pain sometimes. But I don't think he runs chronically and compulsively, which is the definition of addiction I've always worked to. Obsessive interests are also a characteristic of autism. What if he runs obsessively because of that? I realised that obsessive interests, whether for a child with autism or any adult, could be a way of managing high anxiety levels. Immersing yourself in an activity which enables you to feel flow would seem like a sensible way of tackling these overwhelming feelings – better than gambling or drinking at any rate.

The morning of the assessment I was booked to deliver a workshop about diversity to an advertising agency. I'd had about two hours sleep and could barely stop weeping as I made my way to Shoreditch on the bus. I got in touch with a friend on the way in and told her what had happened the day before with the therapist. She helped me to realise that this therapist's view of what was going on was based on limited data points and that she had filled in the gaps. A conspiracy theory perhaps. She said that sometimes experts trust their intuition and that our intuition can always risk being misguided. This was ironic as I was about to run a workshop that taught the dangers of trusting our intuition when recruiting, lest our unconscious biases get in the way. As the week progressed, and I managed to process what had happened in that session, I realised that the therapist had 'caused harm'. I managed to effectively deliver the workshop that morning, but the client complained about me afterwards, saying that I had been brusque and unfriendly with her before and after. Little did she know that I was barely holding it together after being told my husband was an addict the night before and that I was about to go to an autism assessment with my son.

The therapist emailed me a few days later with some resources for me – about addiction, not about autism. She said I'd seemed unsurprised by the comments she'd made. I told her she was mistaken. That I was blindsided. That I'd thought her rude in her sarcastic comments about Steve's fledgling business. To this day, I wish I'd told her that she'd actually caused harm to my family and me. I shouldn't have paid her. The most damage that she did was to destroy further my trust in the experts around me, and this stopped me reaching out for more support for longer than it could have done.

There are a few friends that stand out as people I could trust during this period. I also found it very difficult to open up to others. I think I was scared of seeing my confusion reflected back at me. And there was always the danger that people's responses would mirror the world's prejudices and stereotypes about autism. One person responded by saying, "Oh my god, that's awful". People like this spoke from a place of sympathy – they saw the dark place that I was in and did not want to go near it, staying in their own 'emotionally safe' worlds.

Others joined in with the institution bashing – saying I should trust my own instincts as Leo's mother. To be honest, I encouraged this kind of conversation as it helped to shore myself up and to feel like there were people on my side. But ultimately, it wasn't particularly helpful as it kept me stuck in my denial loop. It also very much operated at a 'thoughts' level, rather than a feelings level – we were discussing my thoughts about the situation and ignoring my feelings. So, in a way, I was only partly seen in these conversations as my feelings weren't discussed or acknowledged.

Other people, I think, wanted to take away my pain and encouraged me from the start to look at the gifts in the situation or just told me that it wasn't that big a deal, that Leo was always going to be Leo to them. From this vantage point, a few months on, I can understand what they were trying to do and it actually resonates hugely. Leo's godfather, Justin, immediately took this perspective and now, a few months later, I am hugely grateful for it. But truth be told, in the beginning, I just wasn't ready to hear this. These kinds of comments, at the beginning, just made me feel like I was somehow wrong for experiencing such difficult feelings. That I should somehow be able to 'do better'. I couldn't see beyond the confusion that I was in at the time, and experienced such well-intentioned messages as people trying to put rose-tinted glasses on the situation, or as people being unable to hold the space for my pain and confusion. It made me feel very, very alone.

For this is what I ultimately craved – someone to hold the space for me to express my pain and confusion without judgement, someone to just understand and recognise what I was feeling. It is such a gift when this happens. And, so rare. I think instinctively we want to make people feel better when they share and, truth be told, it is unlikely, when someone shares something incredibly challenging with you, that a response is actually going to make their situation better. Often what happens instead, when people try to make you feel better, is that you feel more disconnected than before. It feels as though people just don't understand where you are and then you are left with shame about the ferocity and complexity of your emotions on top of the original pain and confusion you were feeling.

So, what is helpful when people share something painful with you? I'm sure that it's personal and people's needs will vary hugely. I do think what we are mostly after is empathy: a simple recognition of our feelings. For me, it was the people who were able to respond with, "That sounds really challenging. You must be feeling really confused and scared right now", that helped me feel less alone. Having my feelings recognised and, even better, validated, was incredibly useful for me at this time. I didn't need people to fix me or make me feel better; I needed people to meet me where I was and to trust that my feelings were valid and real. I didn't trust people to provide this to me and so I was stuck in this paradox whereby it was all I wanted to talk about, yet I didn't trust some of those closest to me to be able to provide what I truly needed.

A few months later, on holiday and struggling with jet lag, I had a vivid and emotional dream. In it, I was struggling with a well-known professional whom I respect hugely, and the people that work with her. For some reason that is unclear in the dream I have the strongest sense that I have been wronged. There's a *Sliding Doors*[19] moment in the dream, in which one part of me shrugs her shoulders, confused, and carries on with life. Another version of me puts up her hand and says, "No! This is not ok". The image in the dream panned out to me sobbing at the back of a huge theatre. At the same time, the 'stronger' me was out front, on the stage, crying with happiness, connection and understanding with the people gathered on the stage. Meanwhile, at the back of the theatre, people I know were coming up to me to see if they could help, some of whom had their own struggles. I brushed them off, telling them they didn't understand and that they have people to help them with their struggles. I was alone. In the dream, I was sobbing and sobbing.

I woke up, confused that I was not sobbing in real life. And felt utterly bereft. I wanted to make sense of the dream and understand its message to me. As I processed it, I saw it as a representation of this very difficult time and the pain that came with

19 *Sliding Doors* is a film in which the protagonist, played by Gwyneth Paltrow, embarks upon two parallel lives following a last-minute rush to catch an underground train. One life derives from her catching the train, the other from her missing the train

it. I had lost my trust in the institutions of the National Health Service (NHS) and the school, leaving me feeling hugely vulnerable. I didn't trust the ability of a therapist to help me navigate my struggle. Equally, I had lost my trust in myself, in my ability to know what was ok and what wasn't ok, and to speak out when things weren't ok. And finally, I had lost my trust in some of those closest to me. I didn't trust them to meet my confusion with empathy and love, and unfortunately the by-product of that was for me to isolate myself further and further. I was left feeling hugely alone.

What could I learn about trust from these experiences, and more specifically, what is needed to rebuild that trust? I think resilience is about the capacity to adapt to change, and it was clear to me that continuing through life without trust in institutions, friends or myself would not be an act of resilience. I think 'getting clear on what is going on' is the first step in the process. Trust is a big word and understanding what sits behind the breakdown helped me to work out how to adapt.

Brené Brown[20], referencing John Gottman's[21] work on relationships, talks about trust being built and broken in the smallest of increments. It is often the smallest behaviours, over time, that create or break trust. I referenced his book *after* having my *Sliding Doors* dream and was surprised to find that he also cited the movie to point out how little moments form important points in a relationship. He claims that too many missed sliding-door moments means that trust erodes and isolation and loneliness take its place. We begin feeling like people aren't there for us. This mirrors exactly how I was feeling at this point in time and I began to think about what my role might be in it. I can't impact on how people treat me,

---

20   Brown, Brené (2012) *Daring Greatly: How the Courage to be Vulnerable Transforms the Way We Live, Love, Parent and Lead*

21   Gottman, John (2011) *The Science of Trust: Emotional Attunement for Couples*

but I do have agency in how I respond to their behaviours, and also in the requests that I make.

Trust-building seems to require vulnerability on my side. I need to have the courage to be able to open up and explain how I'm feeling. When I shut down and hide, it also breaks trust, as I'm not being honest and authentic in those situations. It was really hard to move through this stage together as a couple because Steve and I were experiencing things so differently. Steve truthfully had a more positive outlook from the start on Leo's assessment and diagnosis. There were some gender stereotypes and role-fulfilling at play too in how we moved through things. Steve could see that I was struggling and, for him, that meant he needed to have a different response. One of Steve's common beliefs is that he needs to hold it together emotionally so that the family can be ok and, at times, this puts huge emotional pressure on him. His masculine approach, at this time, was, "'I need to be ok and I need to get on with it". He couldn't see any advantage in 'breaking down' and when I asked him about any feelings of grief, he responded with a quote from the film *Bridge of Spies* – "Would it help if I was?"

I've challenged Steve quite hard on some of these beliefs. I spend a lot of my professional life, as a coach, talking about the need to talk about our struggles. I don't think that 'armouring up' and making out like everything's ok is a helpful way through our struggle. I worry that our high rate of male suicide is in part down to our cultural requirement for men to 'get on with it' and not ask for help. I know Steve would agree with this, however he also cautions against purely looking at things through my own extrovert lens. He believes, as an introvert, that he was processing his feelings and thoughts *internally* during this time period, whereas I really have the need to externalise things so as to make sense of them. As a light-hearted example of this, my younger son Finn is definitely an extrovert. We took him snorkelling on a recent holiday for the first time and he saw hundreds of fish under the water. Every time he saw a fish, he would lift his head up, take his mouthpiece out and tell me that he'd seen a fish! It was almost as if his brain wouldn't process that he'd seen the fish until he'd told someone that he'd seen the fish.

Either way, I think it can be quite difficult for an introvert and an extrovert to move through this struggle together. I had the need to vocalise and talk. My needs weren't always met by the people that I shared with, and sometimes I made up that they wouldn't be met, resulting in me shutting down and the thoughts whirling around my head instead. And I think this increased my anxiety levels hugely. Steve was processing internally and 'getting on with it', although readily admits that 'it' was less of a challenge for him in any case. Ironically, he views the combination of an introvert and an extrovert more positively than I do as he sees his internal work as giving me the space to do my external work. Although I would add that, over the long term, this does lead to him complaining that he doesn't always have a voice in the relationship!

Brené Brown's work in *Rising Strong*[22] provides further clarity. She breaks down the anatomy of trust using the acronym BRAVING – Boundaries (being clear on what's ok and what's not ok), Reliability (doing what you say you're going to do), Accountability (acknowledging it if you don't deliver, making amends), Vault (keeping confidences), Integrity (acting in accordance with your values), Non-judgement (staying out of judgement) and Generosity (believing that people are doing the best that they can). Looking at this list, I lost my voice in saying, "No, this isn't ok". I didn't enforce my boundaries. I also had very high expectations of those around me, and so I think there was also something in there about unmet

22   Brown, Brené (2016) *Rising Strong*

expectations. With the institutions (i.e. school and subsequently the NHS, which would become involved in Leo's assessment), my expectation was that they would be the fountain of all knowledge about autism and understanding my son's needs.

From my present-day vantage point, I can see that this was a bit of 'stealth expectation', as in, it snuck through without me consciously addressing it. It is comforting for us to believe that the experts have all the answers. Yet with autism, so far, they really don't. Whether we're talking about teachers, SENCOs, or those working within the NHS, they largely have the best information that current research is able to provide them with, distilled to a format that is practical for them to work with and apply. My unconscious expectation was that we (society, the experts) truly understood autism. We don't. The people who work within schools and the NHS are also humans and therefore wonderful and imperfect beings. They are doing the absolute best they can with the limited resources that they have at their fingertips. My mind craved the security of absolute trust in the knowledge of the experts, yet I began to lean in to the uncertainty of a new perspective: that we don't yet fully understand autism and that the people working within such organisations are doing the best they can with the limited data and resources available.

My expectation of the therapist was that she wouldn't cause further damage, and would hopefully help me. Instead, she did cause harm. She trusted her intuition readily, and came to a conclusion with which I disagreed strongly. She didn't consider the timing and impact that her revelations might have on me. I didn't need to reframe my expectations of a therapist at all. From my current vantage point, I can see how my own inner voice (even though it took a while) did come out and tell me that this therapist was not the right one for me. I think it is dangerous territory to start distrusting all experts, yet

I also think we need to call people out who claim to know the absolute truth of situations when they have limited data points. At the time of writing this is particularly pertinent – we are seeing what happens when expert opinion isn't trusted in regard to our interpretation of what will happen to the British economy with Brexit, and also in regard to the desperately sad Charlie Gard case (a best interests case in 2017 involving a young boy born with a rare genetic disorder that causes progressive brain damage). Seeing the therapist as an isolated instance of an 'expert' who wasn't right for me is helpful – she is not representative of the whole profession. There are other people out there who can help me.

With my friends too, I was guilty of having stealth expectations. I was expecting them to respond to my needs in a way that equalled that of a therapist! Even I, after years of training in empathy and how to 'hold the space' for people's emotions, frequently get it wrong. I wasn't being clear with my friends as to what I needed and I also wasn't forgiving of them in their imperfection. Struggle is messy and there are no 'rules' about how to move through it and support people through it. Perhaps the best we can hope for is that people try their best to be there, and that we simply honour those who do show up and try. The most dangerous thing is for us is to start isolating ourselves further because of those situations in which our needs aren't met.

My trust in myself began to grow once I had reframed my relationship with the professionals. Once I stopped expecting them to have all the answers, it gave me permission to trust some of my own thoughts and beliefs. Furthermore, the discovery that I could give myself compassion as I struggled was a revelation that shifted my expectations of others, and is explored in greater detail in the 'Self-Compassion' chapter.

And finally, to Leo. Trust seems to be an important function of whether he can truly be himself. He is more readily able to engage with people that he trusts – people who have delivered on his needs and expectations over time. He had a very close relationship with his nursery teacher and I think that was because of her consistency and calmness. He knew what to expect from her and she met his expectations. His reception year teacher was less consistent, although I do believe he did develop a relationship with her. As parents, I think the most important thing for us to provide is a place in which he can belong.

Writing this chapter, I happened to revisit Naomi Stadlen's beautiful work on motherhood[23]. She specifically explores what it is like in that initial stage of having a baby – the overwhelming sense of responsibility and the way that nothing at all can prepare you for it. For me, it is currently like a second, even more powerful wave of responsibility. Indeed, I find myself looking at new mothers in the park, thinking, "Oh my, you have no idea what is ahead". Our responsibility to create a safe haven for Leo has been brought into sharp focus, along with the sheer weight and unknowns within that, and our absolute determination to do our very best by him. No matter what the expectation is of him outside of the home, home will be a retreat to which he can always return and show up as himself. We will have boundaries here, of course, but related to safety and the well-being of all the family. What I want to say to Leo is, "*We will do our best to create an environment here in which you can thrive by being yourself, not by adapting and fitting in.*"

Supporting yourself through loss of trust when your life is diverted.

1   Continue to trust your intuition and your thoughts. Perhaps more easily said than done. However, I believe you will know at some level what is right for your and your child.

23   Stadlen, Naomi (2005) *What Mothers Do Especially When It Looks Like Nothing*

You could use Brené Brown's BRAVING acronym to detail why exactly the trust has been derailed and use this to re-establish it (the acronym works for trust in others as well as self-trust).

2   Get yourself some help from a trusted professional. Find a therapist[24] or a coach. If you cannot afford either of these, find yourself a trustworthy friend who will simply listen to your story. Alternatively, try journaling your swirling thoughts for just fifteen minutes a day. What is important is to find somewhere safe where you can download some of your thoughts.

3   Don't isolate yourself. People out there will want to support you even if they do not, at the moment, know how. Give them a chance and tell them what you need. If necessary show them the animated RSA short *Brené Brown on Empathy*[25] to explain what you need, or this great video *It's Not About The Nail*[26] which encourages people to 'be with' rather than to 'fix'.

---

24 http://www.bacp.co.uk/seeking_therapist/join.php is a directory of counsellors and psychotherapists

25 https://www.youtube.com/watch?v=1Evwgu369Jw

26 https://www.youtube.com/watch?v=-4EDhdAHrOg&t=1s

3

Rolling With Grief

I feel as though I have been very fortunate in my life in that I haven't experienced any truly difficult bereavements and my experience of grief has been few and far between. I teach Brené Brown's Rising Strong curriculum and always felt slightly removed from the section on grief, that I was somehow an imposter claiming to understand it. Then 2016 happened and I realised just how much grief was a theme in my year. My grandma died in the same week as David Bowie and at one point it seemed like you couldn't turn on the news without hearing of another national treasure who had passed away. Of course, grief doesn't have to be about people dying. I think I experienced the loss of trust in institutions, friends and myself as a kind of grief. It was something that I had and that I lost. It was very confusing for me to be experiencing grief about Leo – *"Why would I feel grief? He's the most wonderful thing that has ever happened to me."* Yet, I know what grief feels like and it was definitely grief that I was feeling.

When my grandma, whom we called Totty (her maiden name was Tottenham), died, it wasn't a shock. She was ready to go and I had spent time with her the day before she died in hospital. We had already lost her essence and her power a couple of years before. One of the biggest losses for me, as she died, was of my biggest champion. Put simply, Totty thought that I was amazing. In her eyes, I could do no wrong. It was actually a bit embarrassing at times. In the speech that I gave at her funeral, I thanked her for the unequivocal belief that she had in me and how I wanted to pass that on to my children.

Suddenly though, I had lost my own unequivocal belief in the capability of one of my children. The assessment remains a bit foggy, given how sleep deprived both Steve and I both were. However, it became apparent to me, during the psychologist's questions, that we'd only really been experiencing difficulties with Leo since the summer of 2016. One of the first surprising things to happen was when we were in Lake Tahoe and Leo became obsessed with crazy golf. We literally had to play crazy golf every day of that holiday otherwise our days would have been filled with tantrums and moaning. Anyway, we were on holiday and playing crazy golf together was a fun thing to do. We accommodated it because we believed everyone should get to choose something that we did each day.

Steve and I had different opinions on many of the questions in the assessment. Does Leo show his emotions on his face? I thought he did, Steve thought he didn't. I remember a Brené Brown-inspired exercise where we made Polaroid pictures of us demonstrating a whole range of different emotions. Finn was hilarious and was able to perform exaggerated, almost caricature-like, expressions on request. Leo certainly struggled in comparison with his brother. Does he role-play? Yes, certainly with his brother. On play dates? Neither of us had any idea.

The other notable occurrences of 2016 were that Great Britain voted to leave the European Union and the United States voted in Donald Trump as their new president. I experienced both of these events with grief – I felt like I had lost both hope and optimism for the future. Up until 2016, in my work in the diversity and inclusivity arena, I had felt that, while the work was challenging, I was swimming with the tide. I strongly believed the world was becoming a better place and that people were becoming more accommodating of difference. The political events of 2016 made me question this very core belief of mine. I quickly realised that the world needed the work that I do more than ever, after a brief foray into believing that I was never going to be employed again. But that feeling of being lost has prevailed. I feel as if we (GB, the EU, the United States) were on one path and now it is far from clear which direction we are headed. There is a lot of uncertainty in the air. And a public platform for a lot of hate, fear and division. I grieved the loss of the positive forward momentum.

What concerns me about how we as a nation are working through some of these difficult times is that we don't provide ourselves and each other with the space to feel this pain. The motto is to 'keep calm and carry on'. The only acceptable emotion seems to be anger. And our anger doesn't really seem to be moving us towards a constructive discourse that will actually move us forwards. As I revisit this chapter, it is the twentieth anniversary of Princess Diana's death and I'm reminded of how permission to grieve shifted in this country following that tragedy. Her children, Princes William and Harry, have spoken out eloquently and usefully about their struggle and the support that they have needed. Yet we have so far to go. Grief isn't only about the death of people we love. Any kind of loss can be experienced as a grief – the loss of dreams, of stability, of progress, even of imagined progress. And we just don't give each other the space or time to feel this. I imagine if we don't give each other this space, we can hardly be giving ourselves permission to sit with such difficult feelings. The rush is to get over it, to adapt to it, to brush it off and to rise above it. This stuff *hurts*. It's like we're sleepwalking or numbing some of the hardest feelings and that seems to be a dangerous game.

Could it be that when we are ignoring our pain we are also ignoring our joy? I had a very short period on antidepressants about twenty years ago and the thing I noticed right away was a dampening of enjoyment, as well as the edge being taken off of my pain. Equally, following a retreat during which I opened myself up to some of the more difficult experiences I had been going through, I really noticed that the highs, as well as the lows, were more pronounced upon my return home.

Alongside this, friends of mine were experiencing huge, unfathomable, traumatic loss. A friend from university who lives nearby lost her partner – her partner died after a stroke leaving her to bring up their one-year-old daughter alone. A successful digital strategist whom I had previously coached found out that her three-year old son had a tumour close to his spine. It was strange following her journey on Facebook, as I knew her extremely well having coached her. But she knew little about me. Equally I wanted to reach out and say, "Hey, I know what grief feels like. It's going on over here too". But I couldn't explain my grief and it seemed somehow gratuitous in the face of such tragedy. Before writing this, I read Sheryl Sandberg's *Option B*[27] written after the terrible loss of her husband David Goldberg. As I wrote the opening chapter to this book, I questioned my right to be expressing my feelings. Who are you to feel grief when others are going through greater tragedies? You have still got your child whom you love more than anything else in the world. Who are you to feel grief?

I have realised that our suffering doesn't need to be compared with others' to be real. We all feel. To deny our feelings is to deny the opportunity for us to move through them, leading to the pain

27   Sandberg, Sheryl (2017) *Option B: Facing Adversity, Building Resilience and Finding Joy*

defining our behaviours. For every time that I don't acknowledge this emotion as grief, I can tell you a time when I bit my husband's head off for no discernible reason. Plus, this perspective doesn't help those who are going through unimaginable trauma as they hear the message, "Gosh I cannot even imagine the pain you are going through", ensuring they feel even more isolated and alone.

I found out that this perspective of comparing our situations, and therefore our 'allowed' feelings, is a function of scarcity. Brené Brown (in *Rising Strong*)[28], writes that it is only when we don't believe that there is enough love, compassion and support to go around, that we feel the need to compare our experiences and assess whether they are worthy of our emotions. She calls it comparative suffering. Yet, if we believed there were enough love, compassion and support, this would open up our own permission to feel.

I know what grief feels like, and I know that I have been experiencing grief. I have been struggling to articulate why and partly this is because I was experiencing something called 'ambiguous grief'. I haven't lost anything tangible – I haven't lost a husband or a child. What I have lost are some of my hopes and dreams for our future. I've lost my stability in the now. The novel *This is How It Always Is*[29], about a child who was born a boy but is clearly happiest living as a girl, tells of the moment the parents decided to 'let' Poppy live as a girl. The novel describes how the parents "were slower to adjust" and adds, "They say it is what you never imagine can be lost that is hardest to live without". One of the things the father struggles most with is the ability to use pronouns without thinking. That change was the hardest part for him to live with. In fact, this difficulty reminds him of learning French and finding it *"trés irritant"* that

28   Brown, Brené (2016) *Rising Strong*

29   Frankel, Laurie (2017) *This is How It Always Is*

a French family temporarily living next door could remember which nouns were masculine and which were feminine "when he could not, even though he'd spent a thousand hours studying and they weren't even potty trained yet". Now his whole life was like that.

I thought once the kids started school, things would get easier in our household. This doesn't seem to be what the universe has in store for me. I have lost my image of myself as a mum who has two boys without special needs. Ironically enough, this was a conscious thought I had about three years ago when I was on holiday. Leo kept throwing a ball into the bushes (a theme at that stage in his life!) and another mum thought that he was throwing the ball *over* the bushes to try and get someone to join in with him. I knew otherwise, but she told me, with some sadness, how her sons would never have done that because they had autism. With some shame now, I remember thinking, "Thank goodness I don't have a child with autism".

What has helped is to write down the hopes and dreams that I have lost, and realise that many of those were stealth expectations that might well not have come true anyway. I've lost the chance of happy teenage years with Leo (teenage years are a notoriously difficult time for those with autism). *Who has happy teenage years with their children anyway?!* My son will find school difficult. *Yes, he will, and so do many, many children – including yourself when you were a child.* This may seem a bit of a depressing exercise but it made me realise that, in some instances, I was grieving something that might never have come to pass anyway. In any case, there's no point missing out on some of the joy that might be available to us now, when his challenges are minimal, by focusing on what may happen in the future. Because at the moment, Leo really is ok. It is I who is mired in fog, grief and confusion. Whatever comes with the results of the assessment, it should be clear to me that Leo doesn't have a devastating developmental condition. He has his struggles and is sometimes difficult – like he has always been and like many five-year-olds.

On other occasions, just giving myself permission to feel grief has been expansive. This has been harder than it sounds because my head keeps getting in the way and insisting that Leo is fine (therefore why on earth am I grieving?). Instead of denying it, or questioning whether I should or shouldn't be feeling like this, the most useful thing I could do was to name the emotion and give myself permission to feel it. And yes, just like everyone says, it has felt like a wave. Sometimes, you're on top of it and everything is fine. Then, suddenly, out of nowhere, it comes and crashes over you, pushing you to the bottom.

I also learnt about Martin Seligman's 3Ps in relation to recovering from setbacks in an interview with Sheryl Sandberg in Red magazine[30] (she goes in to more detail about these in *Plan B*). These are Permanence, Pervasiveness and Personalisation, and she talks about how an understanding of these helped her to recover from her husband's death. Permanence is the sense that the setback or causes of the setback are permanent; that you will always be impacted by it and feeling the way you feel about it. Pervasiveness means everywhere. Related to resilience, it is the sense that this event will pervade each and every corner of your life. Personalisation is about the extent to which you feel personally responsible for the event. I realise that I'm doing all three of these. I am seeing both Leo's difficulties and my feelings about Leo's difficulties as permanent, not getting better over time but instead perhaps even getting more challenging over time. I think they will pervade all parts of my life – my relationship with my husband, with my other son, with my work and also with my friends. I am struggling to relate

30 http://www.redonline.co.uk/health-self/relationships/4-things-sheryl -sandberg-taught-us-about-resilence-and-grief

to them. Finally, I am looking for ways to make myself in some way responsible for the situation. I am racking my mind looking for environmental reasons to explain why this has happened, and, beyond that, looking at ways I might not be 'doing enough' at home to support Leo through the situation. I'm quite shocked by this realisation. As someone who speaks publically about resilience, I'm really not adapting to the situation very well! And then I realise I'm even using this as a stick with which to beat myself.

In May 2017, Leo was diagnosed with ASD (Autism Spectrum Disorder). The one to one interview they did with us, alongside a one-hour assessment of him and a questionnaire filled in by the school, brought the psychologist to this conclusion. I was already working through my feelings of grief and noticed that the diagnosis itself didn't create a crashing wave that knocked me under. For Steve, it was a harder conversation. He was forced to confront, for the first time, that the professional world saw Leo as suffering from a 'disorder' rather than a positive character trait. For both of us, it set off a whole new process of learning and discovery.

Supporting yourself through grief when your life is diverted.

1   Any emotion that you are feeling right now is ok. Please don't beat yourself up about any feelings you are having because of the thought that 'worse things are going on in the world right now'. We do not need to make comparisons to give ourselves permission to feel. Your feelings, however messy, are allowed.

2   Give yourself a mental health day. Forward thinking companies are allowing employees time off to take care of their mental health. Struggling through may cause bigger challenges for you in the long term. If you need a day under the duvet watching *When Harry Met Sally*, go gift yourself that.

3   Remember the 3Ps – Permanence, Pervasiveness, Personalisation. A game-changer for me. Examine your thoughts and whether you are unconsciously believing you will feel like this forever, all of the time and that you are at fault for the situation. Moving beyond these negative belief cycles will give you hope. You will not always feel like this, no matter how hard it gets there will continue to be moments of joy and it is unequivocally not your fault.

4

Pulled Under By Shame

I am certified in Brené Brown's work (a professor at the University of Texas, known globally for her work on vulnerability and shame) and so have a good understanding of shame. I've been asked twice, recently, about what drew me to her work with those asking the questions making the assumption that it was because shame was an important theme in my life. That may have unconsciously led me there but the conscious choice was somewhat different. I married Steve in 2012, when Leo was nearly a year old and I was pregnant with Finn. For a wedding present, a dear friend of mine, Anna, bought me a ticket to see Brené speak at Conway Hall in London. It was quite an unusual wedding present as it was only for me (!), and not for Steve. I went along with Anna and experienced quite the epiphany. This lady on the stage was making sense in a funny, articulate and warm way of all of the swirling thoughts that had been going around my head about work and life. She had a decade of research behind her and so immediately appealed to me as someone who found the coaching profession a bit light on its evidence at times. It was there that I first understood the difference between guilt and shame. It took me until I was thirty-three years old to understand this: Guilt is a focus on behaviour whereas shame is a focus on self. Guilt tells you that you've done something bad; shame tells you that you are bad. This is one of the many reasons why, as parents, we are told to focus on the behaviour of our children rather than making them wrong, stupid or naughty. I instinctively saw how feelings of shame had been holding me back in the workplace for years and suspected that the same might be true of many other women.

In 2014, I flew to Texas to get certified in Brené's work. I was quite underprepared when I arrived and had truly trusted my gut instinct that that was where I needed to be right now. It was hard to be away – I'd left a one-year-old and two-year-old behind in London. Everyone was telling me how brave I was leaving my kids behind and it took me until the last day of the course to realise that the icky feeling I had, when people said that, was actually shame. Shame that I was a terrible mother and shouldn't have left them. That I was selfish for pursuing my own interests over their well-being. It was an important lesson about my own shame triggers (bad mum is one the easiest of mine to trigger) and also an important lesson about impact and intent. Just because someone says something that creates a feeling of shame in you, doesn't mean that they intended to shame you. These people congratulating me on travelling to Texas without my babies genuinely meant well and wanted to respect the decision that I made.

I now teach shame in female leadership courses. I talk about how shame underpins many workplace phenomena such as imposter syndrome and perfectionism. Using Brené's curriculum, I teach that shame thrives on secrecy, how to recognise that you are in shame and how to speak of it to someone you trust. I've also realised that being a mother is a shame minefield. You're constantly vulnerable, in danger of somehow exposing yourself. The example I always tell in my courses to explain shame is my John Lewis story. I was in

John Lewis, around the time I went to Texas, buying a birthday present for my husband. I was desperate to finish the conversation I was having with the sales assistant, being at that stage in bringing up children where you rarely finish a conversation. I could see Leo wandering off to the TV department, while Finn remained in his pushchair. I stayed with the sales assistant. Leo was now a fair distance from me but I could see him and also thought to myself, "Nothing bad ever happens in John Lewis". As I hurriedly finished my conversation, and pushed Finn over to the TVs, an elderly man came up to me and said, "I know it's hard but your son is too far away from you". And that moment, I was in shame. My face flushed, my eyes filled with tears and I couldn't speak. I had to gather the children and go straight home, as I was incapable of doing any more shopping. I didn't tell my husband what happened because then he'd also realise that I was a terrible mother and he wouldn't want to leave me alone with the kids. Just thinking about it now provokes a physical reaction in me. Trust me, I know what shame is and what it feels like.

As we moved through this difficult process, I began to notice shame coming up for me. I know the feeling well, and so was well able to identify it. Yet I couldn't make sense of the feeling. I couldn't rationalise it. Why would I feel shame that my son was going through an autism assessment? A friend of mine questioned me outright when I said I was feeling shame. I replied that I thought it was related to the grief that I felt. The feeling that I have lost something, when I have exactly the same, loving, wonderful son that I had six months ago, feels somehow shameful. I was concerned that I was disrespecting him, being unappreciative of him – possibly pushing that 'bad mum' trigger. I remained unconvinced that this was the true explanation, as it didn't quite resonate.

I realised there was something happening on a professional

level too. My work is all about encouraging people to show up as themselves and be valued for it. And here was I struggling to accept a diagnosis of difference in my own family. I couldn't work out if I was rejecting the label because I didn't feel a label would be helpful for Leo, or whether I was rejecting the label because I didn't want a labelled son. I was conscious that the very process that was supposed to be helping my son was bringing out all of my own prejudices and stereotypes. As we met other children with autistic brains, I'd secretly compare and contrast – ensuring Leo came out 'better than' each time. And then I'd feel ashamed that I was creating this idea of what 'normal' was and that I was pleased the nearer that Leo came to this line.

I had talked about gender, ethnicity, broader disability and introversion in my work, yet hadn't talked about neurodiversity. Neurodiversity is still a relatively new term without full consensus. Broadly, it is a term to cover the various neurological differences that occur in people's brains and there is a movement to recognise and respect these as any other human variation. Typically, the term would cover Dyspraxia, Dyslexia, Attention Deficit Disorder, Autism Spectrum and Dyscalculia. It became my ambition to talk about this more through my inclusivity work.

Of course, our experience is a unique one in which Leo's challenges were brought to our attention by helping professionals. For so many other people, the challenge is the other way around. The parents *know* there is an issue with their child and they are reaching out for support from helping professionals. A colleague of mine, Rachael, has a son who has been diagnosed with selective mutism and is undergoing a process of being tested for autism. She has been trying for a while to get the appropriate diagnosis and support for her son. As her son struggled to adapt to life in school, his anxiety manifested as challenging behaviours

– hitting, occasional biting and lots of tears after school at first. This eventually played out at school as throwing things and hitting out at other children as he became increasingly frustrated when he couldn't communicate about events that caused him stress during the day. Rachael and her son have a BAME background (Black, Asian and Minority Ethnic – an abbreviation used in the UK to refer to members of non-white communities) and the school's reaction at first was about 'behaviour management' and felt very negative to Rachael. She very much felt like he was being labelled a naughty child and tells me, "that very much led to me wondering if I was lacking as a parent and that maybe I had got it all wrong and he was just naughty". Fortunately, when she finally saw the speech and language therapist she was told, "Your son isn't naughty, he has an anxiety disorder".

I spoke to Rachael about what it is like to be in the BAME community faced with her son's challenges. I am hugely appreciative to her for causing me to pause and think about the intersectionality of autism and ethnicity. Intersectionality is the overlapping, or intersecting, of social identities and related systems of oppression or discrimination. It would make sense to me that I, as a white, middle-class mum, have a different, one might say privileged, experience. I asked her if she felt the school was quicker to classify her son as naughty than they might have been for a child from a white, middle class background. She replied, "This is a question I wrestle with and my answer changes. I think I am reluctant to say yes because I'm reluctant to accuse anyone of racism (even unintentionally) but deep down I do suspect unconscious bias sometimes happens, and anecdotal evidence certainly points that way. A friend of a friend (who lives outside London in a predominantly white area) had his son excluded from a few nurseries before anyone even suggested he be assessed. It's unfortunate that BAME children, particularly boys, are often associated as being more challenging and less achieving, which no doubt feeds into this bias. I do also think that there is a bias that boys in general are more likely to be challenging, which isn't helped by the 'boys will be boys' mentality that still persists".

There is a belief, backed up by data, that BAME children are diagnosed later, if at all. A 2012 report found that the prevalence of diagnosed autism in pupils of Asian heritage was half of the prevalence in White British pupils[31]. Rachael feels there is a greater stigma around autism in BAME communities and that this might prevent people from asking for help. At the same time, when people do ask for help, there is a sense that it takes a little longer to be taken seriously. A NAS report[32] found that, while many of the challenges BAME parents experienced were similar to those faced by white British families, there were additional challenges around getting a diagnosis. The report found that this was due to schools not noticing the signs of autism and a lower awareness of autism in some BAME communities.

Shame is a key factor. In the report, there is a case study of Pam, a Sikh, who thinks there is a huge amount of stigma in the community of having a disabled child, so parents prefer not to talk about their child's diagnosis. Participants in the NAS research felt that their families were being judged for not being 'normal'. The report says that "Blame was commonly experienced as a view that the child's condition was not natural, and therefore the result of something wrong that someone had done". Some of the participants in the research also felt there was low awareness of, and intolerance towards, autism (as well as other disability) in community spaces such as mosques. The families would in turn avoid those places and

---

31   Lindsay, G. Dockrell, J.Law, J. and Roulstone, S. (2012) "The Better Communication Research Programme: Improving provision for children and young people with speech, language and communication needs." London Department for Education

32   National Autistic Society "Diverse Perspectives"

end up feeling more isolated and disconnected. There is also shame and blame in communities beyond the UK – families who speak with and visit communities in their countries of origin are exposed to different beliefs in those systems, and those messages play on insecurities already held by the parents. Finally, shame showed up as a cultural stigma. There was a belief, for some, in their communities, that autism was caused by bad parenting, accompanied by beliefs that the child's condition might be cured. Furthermore, because there are no high-profile examples of people with autism from BAME communities, people had associations with autism as a white-only condition.

I started to learn more about the history of autism via the big ('in size and in vision'[33]) book *NeuroTribes*[34] and was genuinely shocked by what I found out. In retrospect, and only after speaking to Rachael, I realised how much this book told the white, western history of autism. The common timeline of autism is that child psychiatrist Leo Kanner at Johns Hopkins University School of Medicine in Baltimore, USA, wrote a seminal article in 1943 in which he described "for the first time" eleven children with similar behavioural characteristics which he called "infantile autism". He proposed two essential common characteristics shared by all children with this syndrome. The first was an inclination to self-isolation which he called *extreme autistic aloneness*. The second was a fear of change and surprise, which Kanner called *an anxiously obsessive desire for the maintenance of sameness.*

Silberman (the author of *NeuroTribes*) points out that, in fact, Hans Asperger was working around the same time in Vienna, struggling under Nazi occupation, and had described a similar group of patients. Asperger lectured about a group of children

---

33 Baron-Cohen, Simon (2015) "Leo Kanner, Asperger and the discovery of Autism" *The Lancet* http://www.thelancet.com/journals/lancet/article/PIIS0140-6736(15)00337-2/fulltext

34 Silberman, Steve (2015) *NeuroTribes: The Legacy of Autism and the Future of Neurodiversity*

whom he likened to "absent-minded professors" as early as 1938. These children, despite their social awkwardness and difficulties in social understanding, showed a precocious interest in systems and how things work. It had been thought that these two clinicians weren't aware of each other's work and that they were describing two very different groups of children – high-functioning (Asperger) and low-functioning (Kanner). But Silberman reveals that a diagnostician called George Frankl travelled from Asperger's clinic to Johns Hopkins University in 1938. Silberman's argument is that Kanner heard about these special children in Asperger's clinic in Vienna, found some similar ones in Baltimore, and repackaged them as his own discovery.

Reading Silberman, I feel far warmer towards Asperger's views on autism, which largely saw positive characteristics, than to Kanner's, which focused on the disability. This may have been partly due to the social context in which Asperger was operating his school for special needs. At the time of his research, Nazis were hell-bent on exterminating anyone who didn't fulfil their vision of perfect human beings. Eventually, two hundred thousand disabled children and adults were murdered during the official phases of the child euthanasia and T-4 programmes. Against this backdrop, perhaps it makes sense for him to focus far more on the positive characteristics, in the hope of saving the children. He saw threads of genius and disability inextricably entwined in his patients' family histories and talked about the "social value of this personality type". In a public talk on autism in 1938 he concluded with a radical statement: "Not everything that steps out of the line, and is thus 'abnormal', must necessarily be inferior."

In contrast, Kanner was launching a new field of psychiatry in the States. He needed something to 'cure' with a talking therapy. Whereas Asperger saw the strength of these children in acquiring information systematically, Kanner saw a desperate bid for parental affection. He was working at Johns Hopkins where theories of toxic parenting were particularly pervasive. Psychiatrists Theodore and Ruth Lidz also worked there and were "suspicious of women with professional ambitions; if their dreams were thwarted by motherhood, they predicted, the result would be deep hostility for the children, cloaked in an overweening concern for their welfare". The notion of the "refrigerator mother" was born and quickly caught the public's attention. *Time* magazine drew attention to the high numbers of mothers of children with autism who had college degrees. The now discredited idea was that these children sought solitude as a result of having mothers who exhibited coldness rather than warmth and resentment rather than love. By implicating parenting style, Kanner supplied a raison d'être for autism that struck at the centre of family life.

Bettelheim, another psychologist claiming to want to help treat children, and incidentally a survivor of the Nazi concentration camps, spread this idea further in popular culture. He claimed that "the precipitating factor in infantile autism is the parent's wish that his child did not exist". In *The Empty Fortress* Bettelheim referred to autism as "an illness, a suicide really, of the soul". These ideas have since been discredited, but I wonder how much they still linger in our culture today. My heart breaks for the mothers (and fathers – they too were not immune from Kanner's blame) of the 1950s and 1960s. What must it have been like for these parents to present their child with behavioural difficulties and be told that it was down to them as parents? Shame on top of grief. Confusion on top of fear. And yet it is the parents, not professionals, who have given me hope in the depths of despair this past year.

We are still not immune to such ideas and thoughts, and parent-blaming. Mothers are so often blamed for the behaviour of their children in popular culture today. Celebrity parents get shamed and trolled by online cyber bullies for, what seems to me, fairly innocuous parenting behaviours. At the time of writing Victoria Beckham had been criticised for kissing her daughter Harper on the lips and Chris Evans called out for 'letting' his son wear a dress to a movie premiere. And it's not just the celebrities. A recent US Marie-Claire article, 'The Rise of The Mean Moms'[35], found that 80% of millenial mums said they'd been shamed by other mums – for not breastfeeding, for breastfeeding for too long, for working, for not working. You're damned if you do and damned if you don't. And the underlying theme is not just that you are 'doing' things that are bad for your children, it is that you are a bad parent. It is shame, not guilt.

Steve and I have had a different experience of shame during this period. My observation is that many of the characteristics of autism, when they are made manifest by children in a public space, are the behaviours that people love to shame mothers for – things like unruly behaviour and rudeness, through to the child's apparent inability to do basic things such as dress themselves or feed themselves using cutlery properly. When a child is having a tantrum in Westfield, no one ever looks at the father and asks what he's doing wrong. Equally, we learn, when a child at primary school is unable to dress after swimming, no one tells the father that he needs to teach his child how to get dressed. The assumption is that the mother has failed at this basic parenting responsibility and she is quickly, at the best, given advice and, at the worst, reprimanded, for this situation. Steve agrees fully, "I did care that Leo couldn't get himself dressed – but I seemed to care less than you. I think you were judged more for it and internalised that shame. Mums seem to get the blame for kids missing important milestones."

35   http://www.marieclaire.com/culture/a26300/bully-moms/

We remember together the time I took Leo to a speech and language drop-in session at our local Sure Start Centre, which are government funded centres providing help and advice on child and family health, parenting, money, training and employment. When Leo was two he only had about five words, far behind where he should have been at this age. In retrospect, this is clearly a signal of autism although that wasn't discussed at the time – mainly because he quickly caught up. However, I also had a shaming experience at the drop-in session that day, which convinced me not to return in any case. The first question I was asked by the health worker when I told her about Leo's limited vocabulary was, "Do you speak to your son regularly?". Honestly, I cried for days. Of course, I spoke to my son. In the months running up to this, we had also had a pretty traumatic time. Finn was born fifteen months after Leo with a milk allergy that was undiagnosed for four months. This manifested as him crying – a lot. I was already experiencing feelings of shame for not fulfilling all of Leo's needs while I raced around NHS and private clinics chasing a diagnosis for Finn. The health worker pressed that Bad Mum button and I was flooded with feelings of shame. At the conclusion of the session I was told there was no need to return if Leo's vocabulary improved exponentially over the coming weeks – that is, doubled in week two, then doubled again in week three. I spent week two teaching him how to count to twenty so as to reach this arbitrary goal. Leo picked up his numbers immediately (another huge autism clue in retrospect – he could pretty much count to twenty before putting a three-word sentence together), and I just about convinced myself that he was developing normally. Either way, within a couple of months he was an articulate two-year-old speaking in well-formed sentences. Steve and I told ourselves that this was a reflection of his learning style; he liked to ensure he could do something well before he would try it.

Steve's shame was something different. No one questioned whether he was bringing up his son properly, or judged him for not teaching Leo independence skills. He does believe there is equal, but different, pressure on men, particularly at the school gates. He feels judged and shamed if he loses his temper with the boys – it is particularly painful getting the boys to school in the morning, with a child who can't dress himself, is reluctant to go to school and is not particularly interested in pleasing his teacher by being on time. Many children with autism cannot be rushed and often don't particularly want to go to school. It was implied, from the beginning, that the autism was genetic and most likely to have been carried through the male line. (Later reading up about autism doesn't back up this point, and I can see eccentric, intelligent and absent-minded types on both sides of our families). Steve felt shame that the autism was about his own upbringing, his own lineage and therefore his responsibility. Immediately he saw his Dad in many of Leo's behaviours – Frank has lived in the same house since he was born, has never owned a passport and is methodical about recording the rainfall each day along with the birds seen in his front garden. Steve felt his very being, his existence, was to blame for Leo's challenges.

When working as a maternity coach, supporting women in the transition back to work, one of the most common presenting issues is guilt. Women (*still, in 2017*) tell me how guilty they feel at leaving their children to go back to work, or how guilty they feel at leaving early (usually meaning 'on time') to get back for bathtime or, even, guilty that they don't feel guilty! Guilt seems to be an intrinsic and unavoidable part of being a mum, whether you are working in or out of the home. Again, I think when we are using the word guilt here, we are actually talking about shame. Shame being that intense, visceral feeling that you are not enough and that you don't belong. For me, when I'm in shame, I experience a prickly sensation over my skin, a quickening of my breathing and heart rate and a shutdown of my brain.

I would argue that this isn't just semantics. This is about the potential to change and how you view your very self. If you are feeling guilt about doing something, it suggests that you have made a mistake. That gives you the room to make good that mistake, to do things differently, without sacrificing yourself in the process. It was your action that wasn't great, not you. When you are feeling shame, there is no room for manoeuvre – as it is you, your essence, that isn't enough. Furthermore, shame and vulnerability researcher Dr Brené Brown[36] says shame is highly correlated with addiction, depression, eating disorders, violence, bullying and aggression. Guilt, however, is not. It makes sense that we would want to raise guilt-prone children rather than shame-prone children. And parenting is the greatest predictor of shame or guilt proneness in children[37].

So where do we stand with a diagnosis that calls the child autistic rather than, perhaps, describing their behaviour as autistic? I struggle with labels that encompass the whole person. Perhaps this is only because of the on-going stigma around autism, kicked off by Leo Kanner back in the 1940s. Perhaps if we saw the condition more through Hans Asperger's lens then it would be seen as a more positive label. However, I am still cautious and reluctant to use a word that labels the person rather than the behaviour. In the beginning, Kanner was mapping a distinctive constellation of behaviour. Silberman notes, "in other words, it was the children's behaviour that he was calling autistic, not the children themselves". Perhaps we have got lazy with our language. But calling my son, any child, autistic becomes the dominant definition of self and

36 Brown, Brené (2012) *Daring Greatly: How the Courage to Be Vulnerable Transforms the Way We Live, Love, Parent, and Lead*

37 http://brenebrown.com/2008/07/01/200871blog-series-understanding-shame-html/

I see nothing helpful arising from that. If I was told that my son exhibited autistic behaviour, I think my own shame and grief could have been minimised. I think, in time, that would be an easier concept for my son to wrap his head around. Another use of language that I like is the idea of the 'autistic brain' rather than the 'autistic person'. It's a part of them that works differently, not their self that is broken.

And yet even understanding autism's shameful clinical origins, I still didn't quite feel I had cracked what was causing me such shame. And then I came to a painful realisation. All of my life, I didn't dare to believe that I would end up married and with kids. I come from a history of broken marriages. When we experienced fertility issues, I thought *of course* – somehow believing it was my fate to struggle. I remember vividly walking around Victoria Park (our local park in Hackney) with Leo in his Bugaboo pushchair, marvelling at how everything had turned out. Here I was – about to be married, pregnant with another son and with the most beautiful baby I had ever seen in a pram in front of me. Fast forward to 2017 and I was walking through Victoria Park again, and suddenly thought, "What on earth was I thinking? What made me think that my life might turn out ok? You come from brokenness and your family in turn will be broken." Often being able to understand my emotions helps me to move through them. But this was acutely painful. I was distraught and felt so...broken.

I realised that I was blaming myself for Leo's autism. That my family's mistakes might have created this situation. Had I chosen Steve because unconsciously I was choosing further difficulties and challenges? I briefly danced with all of the vaguely traumatic things that had happened during my pregnancy. I had been on a tube train when the fan unit had exploded, leaving me having a panic attack. Leo's birth had also been fairly traumatic – for me at least! I'm not sure if it would be considered traumatic by the NHS. He'd come down the birth canal sucking his thumb and had got stuck, meaning that an episiotomy and a ventouse were required.

The only thing that helped me out of this mindset was speaking to my husband. I said that I had long believed that I would never get married and have kids. It's still astonishing to me that I did both in my early thirties. I admitted that I didn't feel worthy of the family that we had created and that I was seeing Leo as a symbol of our brokenness. My husband didn't really know how to respond, but I could tell that he listened, that he understood and also that it was so far from his own truth that it was nonsense. I wonder often how Steve is coping with the feeling of shame – truth is, we find it hard to talk about between the two of us. I make up that he must carry a burden from the IVF and from his own genetic heritage. As yet, I haven't seen how that might be impacting upon him.

The Stone Center Counseling Service at Wellesley College in Massachusetts (referenced in Brené Brown's *Daring Greatly*[38]) offers that we have three patterned responses to shame. Some people come out swinging. They use shame to fight shame. Others might hide – when they feel shame they disappear in their communities and from their friends. Finally, some people 'people please' when they feel shame. They try to 'suck up' to people and make themselves liked. Over this period, I had noticed myself hiding away from some of those closest to me, as I didn't want to confront the topic with them. Equally, I found myself blurting it out to people I didn't even know that well. Somehow keeping quiet about the autism seemed to be buying into the thought that it is somehow 'shameful' and, keen to overcome this, I found myself oversharing in possibly

38   Brown, Brené (2012) *Daring Greatly: How Having the Courage to be Vulnerable Can Transform the Way you Live, Love, Lead and Parent*

inappropriate situations. Reflecting on this now, I am still not sure what the 'right' level of discretion might be. I'm sure if my son had broken his leg, I wouldn't have hesitated to tell other people about it. But equally I wouldn't have been worried about seeing some of those closest to me. Another core value of mine is authenticity and sometimes this can be the hardest thing to do with those that you really care for. If I were to be authentic with my closest friends, they would have experienced a crumpled mess. I definitely felt hesitation and unease at the prospect of showing up like that.

Instead I presented a sanitised view to most people of what was going on for me. And I was exhausted. I understand from Brené Brown that authenticity without boundaries isn't authenticity.[39] What I mean is that sometimes we have to censor what we are saying to be suitable for the people with whom we are interacting. Authenticity isn't blurting out your deepest fears to anyone who will listen. And yet our self-management is extremely depleting of our energies. Amy Cuddy writes in *Presence*[40] that "when people lie, they are juggling multiple narratives: what they know to be true, what they want to be true, what they are presenting as true, and all the emotions that go along with each – fear, anger, guilt, hope". Managing this unconscious conflict is exhausting and removes us from being present. Amy Cuddy adds, "Simply put, lying – or being inauthentic – is hard work."

Even after these realisations, my rumble with shame continued. I still couldn't quite let myself off the hook. I knew there was something else going on, an explanation for my feelings of shame that I hadn't quite understood for myself. Why was I feeling shame at the prospect of my son having autism? The rational part of my brain couldn't make sense of it – I knew in my head that there

39 brenebrown.com/authenticity-definiton/

40 Cuddy, Amy (2015) *Presence: Bringing Your Boldest Self to Your Biggest Challenges*

was nothing shameful about it. But I'm aware of how shame feels in my body and was sure I was feeling it. The admissions about family and brokenness had created a lot of clarity but I was sure there was something missing. The more I've considered this, the more I've come to realise that it's a reaction to my own prejudices about disability. Autism, for me at this time, was an ugly word. I thought back to that time on holiday when I met the mother of three children with autistic brains, and how relieved I was that wasn't my world. I also thought of a time when I was brought in to coach some mums of children with disabilities in Islington. I did some great work and connected well with them, but I must admit it was a relief to leave behind their pain and come back into my 'non-disabled' world. This is particularly galling for someone who works in the diversity and inclusivity space. I claim to celebrate difference and to see people's differences as their superpowers. Instead, here I was seeing disability as somehow 'less than' and being barely able to say the word 'autism' out loud without flinching.

Our unconscious biases are the beliefs that we hold about the world unconsciously, and are closely correlated to stereotyping. As human beings we take in vast amounts of data each day and so as to be able to cope with this data, we categorise it. When we think of a surgeon, for example, we might think of a male surgeon. We might believe elderly people to be more forgetful or women to be more empathic and caring. These are all stereotypes and it is a universal human trait to stereotype. You literally cannot be human and not make use of stereotypes. I realised I held hugely unhelpful stereotypes in my head about autism. I, unconsciously, held a belief about an unresponsive, self-centred, uncommunicative child who was incapable of empathy or connecting with those around him. When people were suggesting my son was autistic, I was unconsciously believing they were saying that my son was all of these things. Which he clearly isn't. But more importantly, there was a hot flush of shame associated with my child being any of these things *because of my inability to be with disability.* I wondered if I would ever be able to 'befriend' the autism, to see it as his superpower or at the very least, be able to say the word out loud without shuddering.

How to stop shame from pulling you under when your life is diverted.

1   Speak shame. It is my mission, along with the rest of the global Daring Way™ community, to kick start a global conversation about shame. We just don't talk about it. And yet, we all experience it. Brené Brown's shame resilience technique is to recognise you are in shame, understand your shame triggers and speak shame with someone you trust. This won't make you resistant to shame, but it will support you in moving through this difficult emotion with more ease.

2   Let go of comparison. My friend, comparison is not going to serve you here. How your child is vs other children. How you are coping vs how other people are coping. Focus on your child and what he/she needs. Focus on you and what you need.

3   Repeat after me, *"Having a child with autism does not make you a bad parent. And it does not mean that your child is not worthy of love and belonging in this world either".* We know this. And sometimes we just have to remind ourselves.

4   Separate guilt from shame. Focus on the behaviours rather than on the self, whether that is within the mistakes that you will inevitably make or whether it is related to your child. Consider what language you want to use within

your family relating to autism, and what is helpful for you. Switching 'autistic child' to 'child with an autistic brain' was hugely beneficial for me.

5   Create a mood board of inspirational role models. When you first research autism, you may feel floored by the quantity of distressing stories out there. This doesn't have to be your story, yet if you only see those negative stories you may inadvertently internalise them. I created a mood board of positive role models – some of whom our family know and some of whom are in the public eye. I have been adding to this over time and it is a huge source of strength and inspiration to me.

5

Shifting My Perspective

It's painful to admit this, but I began to realise about half way through the year that one of the biggest difficulties in our lives was me. To be clearer perhaps, rather than me, it was my way of thinking that was getting in our way. I had taken Leo and Finn to football in the local park over consecutive Saturday mornings in the late spring. Every Saturday morning they would ask to go, and every Saturday morning upon arriving they would refuse to join in the football and, instead, make 'bonfires' (not lit of course!) out of sticks they found lying around.

The third week of this happening, I started to feel pretty irritated by it. To get them dressed, out of the house and into the park by 9am on Saturday morning felt like quite an effort. The least that they could do was to join in! I begged, I cajoled and I pleaded. This time at least, I stopped short of bribing. But they were clear that they didn't want to join in. Suddenly, I was feeling all of that shame, failure and loss all over again. Shame that I must somehow be a 'bad mum' who can't bring up children to be like everyone else's children who just join in the damn football. Failure as, for the third time running, *I've* failed to get them to join in. And the ambiguous grief that accompanies the loss of an unconscious dream. Simply put, I thought I'd be a mum who could drop her kids off at football on a Saturday morning and enjoy a run and a coffee. Well maybe a coffee…

Tears were pricking my eyes as I stood by the trees – luckily, it was a sunny day and I had some shades on. A friend saw that I was struggling and came over to me. At this point, I thought to myself she must be an angel put on earth to take care of me. She sent her husband off to buy us all some coffee and reminded me that Leo wasn't the first five-year-old to not want to join in at football. "This doesn't have to be about autism, my love." She was right of course – but then there was more. "Rox – look how happy your two children are and how miserable you are. Leo is fine. He's having a brilliant time in the park in the sunshine on a Saturday morning. What a joyful experience they are having." I sighed, looked at them both and had to agree again. They were fine. Leo was having a brilliant time. It was my mindset that was causing me the pain – not Leo's actions. There will be plenty of times when Leo's actions do cause me pain, but this didn't have to be one of them.

After football had finished, Leo did have an autistic moment. He got fixated on his friend coming around to our house. For many reasons, this wasn't a great idea right then – our dog hadn't been taken out for a walk yet and his friend is scared of dogs, and the friend's parents wanted to get home and get changed before a school fete that afternoon. Plus, we couldn't always be changing our plans to accommodate Leo's desires. He sat down on the floor and refused to move. Knowing I was wobbly this same friend stayed with us all. She showed Leo her diary and booked a play date for her son and him a week later, during the school holidays. He was mildly interested but still refused to move. She remembered how much Leo loves geocaching (an outdoor recreational activity in which participants use a Global Positioning System to find hidden containers called caches) and got her phone out again to show him the nearby caches. She asked him if he would like to show her a nearby cache. His face lit up and we all headed over to a bench in Victoria Park Village, a leafy and gentrified cluster of shops and cafes in our corner of Hackney, where one of his favourite caches is hidden. My friend, Leo's friend and her husband stayed with us all of the way – without looking irritated or put out in the slightest. I was apologising for the detour and they were all enthusiastic and excited about seeing the cache. The change in perspective for me? A change in plans, or a compromise even, doesn't have to be a disaster and equally doesn't mean that my children are 'getting their own way' all of the time. If I get stuck in that perspective, I'm harder on Leo and everyone is more miserable. Also, when tough things happen, sometimes the universe sends along an angel to support and help you along. *Look for the helpers.*

This idea of 'changing your perspective' is contained within many coaching techniques and models. I trained with the Coaches Training Institute and it is at the core of balance coaching. The premise is simple – sometimes you can't change your situation, yet you are always capable of changing your perspective about a situation. Stuck in a queue? You can't change the fact that you're stuck in the queue. But you are at choice as to whether you decide to find that queue irritating or a welcome breather to stop and slow down for ten minutes.

I think the important thing in this approach is to ensure you firstly recognise the suffering that sits within the situation. Too often, I have shared something painful with my husband and he has replied, "How could you think differently about that situation?" I get that he wants me to feel better and that he's trying to help. Yet it's really frustrating. I have shared something incredibly painful in a bid for connection and I end up feeling more alone and isolated, as though my pain hasn't been heard or understood. The approach also risks neglecting responsibility for some of the very real situations that people might find themselves in – such as poverty, unemployment, and illness. I do some work with Bump Buddies, a peer to peer maternity support network in Hackney. There are women seeking support with incredibly difficult situations – they might be pregnant, with no housing, no money and no recourse to public funds. It is extremely damaging to expect such individuals to simply shift their perspective on their situation. Shifting their perspective is not going to ensure their baby has somewhere safe to sleep at night. Sometimes the difficulties in which we find ourselves are systemic and absolutely require those who can to intervene and change the situation.

Yet my ability to remove my own expectations on myself, and also on Leo, has been pivotal to our moving through this. Unrealistic, stealth expectations will bring us all down. Getting rid of the 'should haves' is equally important. *He should have joined in at football. I should have prepared him for this activity better.* All the time Leo is happy, I certainly have the opportunity to look at him and see a happy five-year-old. That's my choice.

I still had moments of questioning Leo's diagnosis, yet felt my perspective shifting here too. It's a problematic situation to be in, partly because denial is one of the very first characteristics of adapting to change. The NHS tests give a numerical result, but this is based on very subjective data. For a start, Steve and I disagreed on a number of the questions in the interview that we had. And would have given different answers three months later. The assessment that Leo attended seems to be unable to distinguish between a child who won't do a requested task and a child who can't do a requested task. In fact, David Mitchell writes in The Guardian[41], "It seemed that a bright examiner capable of engaging a child's attention would arrive

---

41   https://www.theguardian.com/society/2017/jul/08/david-mitchell-son-autism-diagnosis-advice

at a different result from a tired, unimaginative examiner – implying that DISCO's truest measurement is the tester's skill at administering DISCO." (DISCO is the test that has been designed and evaluated to assist in the diagnosis of individuals with a query of an Autism Spectrum Disorder). Autism seems to defy definition and autism symptoms vary hugely between people and also over time. There is a common saying, "If you've met one person with autism, you've met one person with autism". The lack of rigorous, certain classification along with the nature of Leo's autism (high functioning) opened the door for a huge amount of questioning and uncertainty.

I became aware over time that my resistance to his diagnosis was making things worse for me. When I accepted he had autism, I would feel calmer and more at peace. When I didn't accept he had autism, I would feel very anxious and overwhelmed as I struggled continuously in my head with all the arguments to confirm or deny the diagnosis. In a parallel, but opposite, process, if Leo was doing well, I would find my well-being improving. If he was struggling, or was 'triggered' or 'deregulated' as we started calling it, I was struggling. The outcome of these two processes was that I never really gave myself the opportunity to be ok.

I was resisting the autism diagnosis in that I was resisting the label that the professionals wanted to put on him and all of the meanings associated with that label. This showed up for me as hyper vigilance about his behaviour. I would also obsessively read about misdiagnoses on the internet and order books from Amazon. One rabbit hole was a book called *The Einstein Syndrome*[42] – about a group of children who started to speak rather later in life than one would anticipate, and yet grew up to be bright, high achieving adults. Wouldn't one prefer to have a child with Einstein syndrome rather than autism? This process felt busy in my head, as if I was

42   Sowell, Thomas (2001) *The Einstein Syndrome: Bright Children Who Talk Late*

constantly hungry for new information, yet I was just taking the parts of these stories or research that fitted with my own story.

I asked myself how this resistance was serving me. Interestingly, I noticed that it was serving me to believe that I was leaving no stone unturned in my quest to find the best support for my son. I was using the resistance to prop up my desire to be the perfect mother. There are a lot of unknowns about autism and was it perhaps healthy to have a small dose of scepticism and questioning?

However, the resistance was also clearly not serving me in many ways too. I was tired, anxious and overwhelmed. Crucially, my own need to put a binary label on Leo was stopping *me from truly seeing and accepting Leo as he is.* I was looking to confirm or deny a label and missing seeing him. All of that energy I was spending on reading and obsessive thought patterns could be simply spent with him.

As I thought more about this, I realised a different perspective was available to me. It actually doesn't matter whether Leo has an autism diagnosis or not. That isn't what's important here. What's important is ensuring Leo has the right support and parenting style for his needs. Period. Just like any other child. And just like any other parent, I was worrying – and will continue to worry – about what the best thing is for him. And that's fine. Questioning whether he's getting the right support, rather than obsessively questioning his diagnosis, opens me up to seeing him and what he actually needs, and then investigating what support is available. What is Leo struggling with right now and where could an intervention be helpful? At its simplest, what works? What works when we're trying to get him dressed? What works when he's consumed with anger? The diagnosis for us gave us access to some workshops where we'd get further ideas about 'what works' and could build our own strategies and interventions based on what works for him.

Beginning to shift your perspective when your life has been diverted.

1   It's time to start questioning those thoughts of yours. Write them down and then examine them like an A-level examiner. Are these thoughts actually true? Have some 'untruths' snuck their way in? Ask yourself, "What is important here?"

2   Challenge yourself to find a perspective that serves you. What perspective are you sat in right now? Is it serving you? Are other perspectives available to you that might serve you better?

3   Focus on 'what works'. You'll be given countless advice and recommendations as you move through this process – some of it may well be useful and some of it might be totally unhelpful. As with all parenting advice, take it with a pinch of salt. There is no one size fits all approach for autism, just like there is no one size fits all approach for parenting. Try what feels right for you and focus on what works for you and your child.

6

Offering Myself Self-Compassion

My journey to greater self-compassion has been an interesting one with more than a little help from the universe along the way. I was introduced to the work of Kristin Neff via Brené Brown. Kristin Neff is an associate professor at the University of Texas at Austin's department of educational psychology. She is the author of *Self-Compassion*[43] and has made it her life's work to understand this topic, creating the Self-Compassion scales along the way. Self-compassion is a module in the Daring Way™ intensives that I run, and so it has been important for me to understand what self-compassion is so that I can teach it to others. I have noticed often that the female leaders whom I coach speak to themselves in a way that they wouldn't even speak to their worst enemies. They are so nasty and mean to themselves! Put simply, self-compassion is about speaking to yourself as you might speak to a close friend. Kristin Neff also defines it as recognising your own suffering and realising that it is part of the human experience. For example, if you put on ten pounds, the self-compassionate person might look at themselves in the mirror and say, "Gosh, it's true you've put on some weight there. That's really tough to realise. But remember

---

43   Neff, Kristin (2011) *Self-Compassion: The Proven Power of Being Kind to Yourself*

that so many women struggle with their weight and feel terrible they put on some weight."

I had never recognised in myself this almost abusive self-talk that I began to witness in my clients once I started asking them about their internal dialogue. I also had an initially ambivalent view of Kristin Neff (which is embarrassing to admit to now, having met her and thoroughly benefitted from her research!) In her videos she's surrounded by Buddhist paraphernalia and is speaking in a really soft and gentle tone. It's not really my style and I found it hard to relate to. In retrospect, I was being horribly judgemental about something I didn't know much about. Many times, female leaders I worked with were also sceptical, when I showed videos of Neff's talks to them. They couldn't relate to her message and either felt that their critic's voice had been so instrumental in getting them to where they were that they didn't want to lose it, or they sensed that their negative self-talk was so hardwired it seemed futile to try and shift it. In May 2016, I attended Courage Camp, which is the global community meet up for all of those certified to deliver the Daring Way™ work. I was super excited about going and, as ever, it was incredibly difficult being away from my kids. Kristin was the keynote speaker on the last day of the meet up and shared her work on self-compassion.

She began with the science. The physiological underpinnings of self-criticism are your body feeling threatened – which produces cortisol and adrenalin. You don't need me to tell you quite how damaging these are in large quantities for our bodies. The physiological responses are trying to attack the problem but in actual fact these stress hormones are attacking ourselves because we make ourselves the problem. In contrast, the physiological underpinnings of self-compassion are found in the mammalian caregiving system. Physical warmth (giving a hug), gentle touch and soothing vocalisations all produce oxytocin and opiates in our system. Also, when you are compassionate the reward centres of the brain light up. Self-compassion literally gives our body the resources to be able to hold our own pain.

When we think about our success being driven by our own self-criticism and harshness, you cannot help but wonder at the cost of that. Sure, we may be driving our external success with promotions, pay increases and getting that mortgage. But what is the cost of that to our physical and mental health? And is it truly sustainable? We know that women seem to be more sensitive to the stress hormone cortisol than men (as detailed in Arianna Huffington's *Thrive*[44]). On a professional basis, I was starting to think I needed to take this all a bit more seriously.

Then, at Courage Camp, Kristin began to talk about her son who has autism. (This was six months before I got blindsided by Leo's form teacher). She described an incident in a shopping mall when he was having a huge meltdown. Rather than rush to his aid, she spent a short while attending to herself first – putting her own oxygen mask on first if you like. She gently stroked her arm and reminded herself how tough it is to be out in a public space when a child has a tantrum. She checked in with her emotions and noticed that, indeed, she was feeling pretty anxious and stressed right now. She told herself that it was totally normal to feel like that and mothers all over the world have found themselves in such a position of adversity. She was not alone. Once she had completed this 'self-compassion break', she told us, she began to attend to her son.

The impact of taking this time out for herself was huge. It gave her the resources to be able to deal with the difficult moment. However, for her son, it was perhaps more astonishing. She told us that her son started to 'mirror' her. A natural human reaction is to

44   Huffington, Arianna (2015) *Thrive: The Third Metric to Redefining Success and Creating a Happier Life*

mirror the emotions and behaviours of those around us. Typically, she might mirror her son's response, feeling anxiety, stress and overwhelm. Instead, as she approached him with calmness and self-compassion, she began to sense that he was mirroring her. He slowly started to calm down, his breathing slowed and his flailing around decreased. Gradually they were both calm again, right there in the shopping mall.

This idea of a 'self-compassion break' seems to me to be a game changer for the parent of a child with autistic tendencies who is prone to a meltdown[45]. Or any parent who experiences struggle with their children. Or anyone, actually. It is simply an exercise that you can use, at any moment of struggle, to support yourself and create a shift in your perspective, approach and physiology. The first thing is to notice that you are suffering, and literally say to yourself, "This is a moment of suffering.". This is mindfulness – noticing what is happening to you. You might equally say, "Shit, this hurts", or "This is bloody hard" if that feels more natural to you. The second thing is to remind yourself that suffering is a part of life. You might say, "That's common humanity", or "Other people feel like this". At this point Kristin recommends using supportive touch – you might put your hands to your chest or stroke your hand. Whatever works for you. The final part is to say something kind to yourself. Ask yourself, "What do I need to hear right now to express kindness to myself?" Maybe it is, "May I forgive myself" or "May I be patient" for example. It is a really simple strategy to employ when you are feeling overwhelmed and that overwhelm threatens to make an already bad situation worse. It certainly feels weird and forced the first few times that you do it. But it totally does resource you up and increase your capacity for dealing with whatever shit is being thrown at you.

And here's the intriguing bit for me. This was six months

---

45   You can find it on self-compassion.org (Kristin Neff's website) which is an excellent resource

before I had the conversation with Leo's form teacher. I had never had a conscious thought in which I raised the possibility that Leo might have autistic tendencies. Yet, I started ugly crying at Kristin's story. The tears were streaming and I was struggling to breathe. My shoulders were shuddering and I was flooded with emotion. To this day, I am unable to explain the visceral response that I had to her talking. Something happened in that room that I cannot quite explain or understand. But I knew that I needed to pay attention.

Fast forward a few months and we were caught up in the confusion and 'not knowing' that the road to an assessment brings. I received an email telling me that Kristin Neff and Chris Germer (clinical psychologist, co-developer of the Mindful Self-Compassion programme and author of *The Mindful Path to Self-Compassion*[46]) were offering a week's intensive course on self-compassion in Amsterdam in the summer of 2017. I trusted that my intuition knew that this was exactly where I would need to be come June and signed up. I hardly thought it through because I knew my mind would come up with a thousand reasons why I shouldn't be in Amsterdam spending a week working on a concept that I'm not particularly intrigued by rationally. In fact, three colleagues decided to join me – my supervisor, my co-lead for the Daring Europe and Africa community and a GP who came on one of my Daring Way courses with whom I had connected immediately.

Before I went away, I was still so averse to the idea of self-compassion that I actually didn't tell some people where I was going. "Oh, I'm training in Amsterdam", I muttered vaguely, knowing full well that people would infer that I was delivering an Accelerate programme to professional women (training I often deliver in Amsterdam for ECC, a coaching consultancy I do associate work for). My husband only really found out what I was doing because

46   Germer, Chris (2009) *The Mindful Path to Self-Compassion: Freeing Yourself From Destructive Thoughts and Emotions*

he joined a friend and me for drinks after work the Thursday before I left for Amsterdam and I had opened up to her about the programme. Before arriving in Amsterdam, I was anxious and slightly fearful. I also knew I was useless at mediation and made up that it would be a week of me falling asleep attempting to meditate. The irony of my shaming self-talk demonstrating to me my own need for a course on self-compassion was not lost on me.

We were asked to set our intentions at the beginning of the workshop with a reflective practice. What came up for me, immediately, was, "to love myself". Which was a bit of a surprise – and also slightly scary. Kristin then asked, "What really brought you here?" I thought to myself: that it is to be able to be fully present and supportive for Leo when he needs it. What if, in those difficult moments, I could take care of myself and then support him, rather than being caught up in shame and judgement about his behaviour, my behaviour and my parenting? I was there to be a better parent to both of my children. It's funny the lengths I'll go to to be better at my job or better at parenting, pretending I'm not investing time and energy in myself. Straight away I noticed the shame-based component of my objective. I was saying that I was somehow not a good enough parent and that I wanted to change myself, rather than focusing on the behaviour. In what I hoped was a self-compassionate response, I shrugged and let myself off the hook.

One of the basic components of self-compassion is to treat yourself as you would a good friend. If a good friend was told her child had autism, what would I do? I hope I would tell her that I was there for her, I would recognise her pain, fear and uncertainty and I would listen to her without judgement. When I reflect on how I treat myself, I notice that while I am 'good' at recognising the emotions I am feeling, I put myself under pressure to move through them in a way that I just wouldn't expect from someone else. I would tell a friend that there is no right way to move through grief, yet I tell myself that it's about time I stopped feeling that because I have two beautiful and healthy sons. Someone in the workshop noticed that they sometimes struggle to be compassionate to those who are closest to us. Kristin suggested that this is a common occurrence – to be the least compassionate to the people that are the most integral in our lives. And that this is linked to how threatened we are by their struggles. Our defence system might be more likely to kick in when we see our partner struggling, rather than a colleague at work, for example.

Kristin Neff has carried out and also collated a lot of research addressing people's misgivings about self-compassion. For those that worry that their inner critic gives them the kick to be successful in life, she pulls out research that shows a correlation between increased self-compassion and an increased ability to pick yourself back up again after a failure and try again. For parents of children with autistic brains, her research has shown that increased self-compassion is correlated with decreased levels of stress; in fact, self-compassion was a bigger predictor of the ability of a parent to cope with their child's special needs than the severity of the autism.

The week consisted of us learning more about the research and theory around self-compassion, and also learning both formal and informal practices. The formal practices were meditations designed to foster greater self-compassion. The informal practices were techniques you could use 'in the moment' when you perhaps needed a bit of extra support. The 'self-compassion break' that Kristin described in Texas is one of these – taking a break in a moment of struggle to offer yourself some self-compassion; that is, to recognise your suffering, communicate kindly with yourself about it and remind yourself that your suffering is part of the suffering of everyone. The idea is that you are *always* there to provide support for yourself, and so if we can get better at doing that we will be able to deal better with the difficulties that life throws at us.

We did some really difficult work over the week about meeting some of our difficult emotions with self-compassion. Fairly early in the week, I realised that the word self-compassion is related to suffering. It's how we treat ourselves when we are suffering. The week was therefore not going to be a lovely, relaxing week of being rather nice to myself! This thought hadn't occurred to me before going there. We were going to be dealing with suffering and addressing how we communicate with ourselves when that comes up.

That said, one of the hardest moments of the week for me was when we were doing quite a simple early morning meditation. We were encouraged to think of someone who might need our compassion and I immediately thought of my children who were struggling at home – perhaps because I was away, but also perhaps because it was the last week of the school year and there was a lot of upheaval and uncertainty for them. We were encouraged to breathe out compassion for them and breathe in compassion for ourselves. Straight away I struggled – if I was truly compassionate about my children, surely, I would be there with them. I attempted to continue the meditation but found it increasingly difficult. Internally, I was berating myself for not being at home. I was blaming myself for their struggle. Breathing out compassion for them seemed utterly futile and, in any case, if I was the cause of their struggle by being away, it also seemed pretty fake. Once the meditation finished and a conversation about it began, I found my emotions overwhelming.

Chris Germer has a wonderful diagram of three concentric circles detailing how we are with our emotions. The first, inner one, is labelled 'safe' – here, we are with our emotion and feeling it, and we feel safe in doing that. The middle one is labelled 'struggle' – being with our emotion feels hard, we are struggling to somehow manage and contain it. The final, outer circle is labelled 'overwhelmed' – the emotion is overwhelming to us. I was firmly in overwhelm and was unable to remain in the room. I slipped out of a side door.

One of the classroom assistants came out to talk to me. Handily, she was a trained psychologist and was wonderful at just sitting with me and holding the space for my overwhelm. Slowly I was able to speak again and tried to make sense of what was going on for me – how hard it was being away, how the kids were struggling, how I was blaming myself. She encouraged a conversation about self-compassion, pointing out that leaving the room, when I couldn't cope, was self-compassionate. I recognised that I was overwhelmed and did something kind to myself. We talked about other mothers who are away from their kids (thereby touching on the common humanity of my struggle). Kristin herself has a son with an autism diagnosis and must also be struggling with being away. How do all these women do it? I noticed I am so judgemental of mothers being away from home for a long time and really that is a function of my own difficulty and struggle with being away. The lightbulb moment for me came when the assistant kindly suggested, "Look at what you are showing your children. That it is hard to choose our own path in life. That we can't keep everyone happy when we are following our own path."

Perhaps part of the problem when we are not kind to ourselves, is that we are not kind to other people either. I have long thought that we are most judgemental of other people in the areas in which we are most judgemental, and insecure, of ourselves. Learning to be kinder to myself has been a huge part of my resilience journey. Leaving Amsterdam, I noticed the week after the retreat that I felt more alive. The highs were definitely higher. I noticed and experienced joy in a way that I hadn't felt for months (maybe years).

I also really felt the harder emotions too. But in a way that felt manageable. I knew I had the resources, on my own, to be able to stay safe and move through them. I continue to be crap at meditating. The informal practices, however, have really stayed with me. I have been wearing a self-compassion bracelet on my wrist, and it has reminded me to consciously be self-compassionate when something hard happens. I literally just touch the band if I notice that I am struggling, and say something kind to myself and look for the common humanity in the situation. It has served to give me a pathway to move through what is happening.

How to offer yourself self-compassion when your life is diverted.

1   Treat yourself like you would treat a good friend. What would you say to a friend in a similar situation? How would you recommend she or he looked after themselves? Take these kind words and thoughtful advice and apply them to yourself.

2   Learn the self-compassion break for those difficult moments. In this you notice your own suffering, offer yourself some kind words and soothing touch and, finally, remind yourself that suffering is part of the human experience and there are many others struggling with finding themselves on an unexpected path too.

3   Do something just for you, regularly. Many parents lose themselves through this struggle and my belief is that it is important to hold on to your identity and the things that you love. While therapy was hugely helpful for me, it was further down the line when I decided to go horse riding each month (something I have longed to do since childhood), when I really started to feel like myself again.

7

Building Community

I'm frequently reminded of Brené Brown telling me, "If you want to do something counter cultural with your life, you need people in your support section." When I am using her work to support people in showing up, living brave and being seen, I have them draw themselves in an arena with seats around them. We work through who is sitting in those seats – in the critics' section and also in the support section. Getting clear on what critical messages you might receive when doing something seems to help people prepare for them and be ready to deal with them. However, we cannot just have our eyes on the critics' section. We also do well to look towards our support section, the people that are championing us, supporting us and encouraging us to truly show up.

As I have been hiding from some of my closest friends, I am finding my own support section a little light on the ground. I have mixed experiences with people's responses when I do blurt out our news and our struggle. By now, I have divided them into categories. There are those that respond with horrified sympathy, "Oh my goodness, that's so awful." I pretty much want to punch them in the face. Others tell me that Leo will always be Leo and I shouldn't worry about it at all. I get that they're trying to be helpful, and it's great that they don't intend to view Leo through the label he's been given, but I continue to leave these interactions feeling somehow unseen. How can they not understand that this is intensely difficult for me? There are others who try and persuade me to look at the positives of the situation. "You can't keep getting upset about this Rox. He's an amazing boy with super powers. Please stop crying." And then there are the 'at leasters' – "At least you've found out now", "At least it's high functioning autism", "At least you can now put a plan together". They're right, these are all things to be grateful for, but I still pretty much want to punch them in the face too.

Ironically, what is missing from these situations is empathy. Empathy is feeling with people whereas sympathy is feeling for people. "Empathy fuels connection. Sympathy drives disconnection"[47]. It is difficult when faced with somebody's heart-wrenching news to find the right thing to say. I've certainly been guilt of the 'at leasts'. The people who have made me feel the most supported are those who have recognised my suffering in an empathic way, rather than a horrified sympathetic way. They say, "That sounds tough" and walk alongside you, rather than, "Oh my god that's awful", as they slowly back away. But at a time when I was isolating myself, those people that looked me in the eye and said, "Things must be really tough for you right now", were those who enabled me to feel seen and understood. One person even said, "Rox, I just don't know what to say to you right now, but I am here alongside you," which I also appreciated.

Empathy, according to the Merriam Webster dictionary, is "the action of understanding, being aware of, being sensitive to, and vicariously experiencing the feelings, thoughts and experience of another"[48]. A lot of people tell me they can't possibly imagine

47   Brené Brown in this RSA short on Empathy: https://www.youtube.com/watch?v=1Evwgu369Jw

48   https://www.merriam-webster.com/dictionary/empathy

what I'm going through. In some ways, I don't want them to imagine. Yet, telling me they can't imagine my feelings creates more disconnection and isolation. I leave thinking, "Wow things must be really, really awful!" The thing is that these people have experienced struggle, they've had times when they've been worried about their children and few people get to our stage of life without experiencing some kind of grief. Yes, they haven't experienced exactly the same struggle that I am facing, but they have experienced the same emotions. Empathy is about identifying these emotions and moving through them alongside the person who is struggling. This is why it is such a vulnerable, depleting and yet connecting experience.

And sometimes there is a role for connecting with people who have been through a similar experience. I slowly began to connect with the parents of other children with autism. Before the diagnosis I met one family whose son goes to the same school as Leo, although he's in Finn's year (and has become one of Finn's friends). It was hard to see the pain that his mother was in, yet it was also vaguely reassuring to not be the only person who has to go through this. One of the unique characteristics of autism is the differences between the children. Finn's friend has different characteristics to Leo – for example he is less able to tolerate eye contact, at least when he is with me. What we are experiencing is in some ways so different. Yet she also tells me about grief, the months of uncertainty and the pain of the diagnosis. Because they present so differently, we do cling on to a bit of hope that Leo, because he is so different to her son, might not have autism, which really isn't so helpful for us. (I know my friend too has her own denial moments). However, in her I hope I have found a friend for life, not just because we have found ourselves in this club that nobody wanted to be a member of – the parents of children with autism.

One thing my new friend tells me about is her struggle at some of the community meet ups for parents of children with autism in Tower Hamlets. Once you get a diagnosis, you get given a ream of paperwork and invites to coffee mornings, occupational therapy appointments and seminars. The challenge is that her son and Leo have high functioning autism. The groups encompass such a broad spectrum that it can be difficult to find someone in the same situation as you. Some children with autism don't speak or can't pick up a pen. Leo, on the whole, 'passes'; that is, he does not noticeably display autistic characteristics when you initially meet him. This presents its own challenges, as people are less able to adjust their expectations of him and sometimes simply see 'disobedient child'.

I was working abroad at the time of the first coffee morning in Hackney that Steve and I were invited to, and so Steve went to it alone. He reported back in a similar vein. We were struggling with persuading Leo to get himself dressed and to write on single lined paper, rather than double lines, at the time. Parents there had older children who wouldn't (or couldn't) speak, pick up a book or a pen. Steve told me he felt somewhat fraudulent in his attendance and also inadvertently became the shoulder for other people in the group, with far more challenging situations, to lean on. Online forums proved equally challenging. A good reminder to me that Leo's challenges are mild, online forums can also be a scary and anxiety inducing place. As I have already mentioned, I don't really see the value in worrying about his teenage years now, while he is enjoying life and we enjoy a good relationship with each other.

One night, out enjoying some much needed wine, my new friend and I realised that the answer might be right under our noses at the school. We had already been told by the SENCO that there seems to be a cluster of children with high functioning autism in East London – possibly because it is genetic and their parents might be working around Old Street or Shoreditch in the tech industry or in the City. We canvas opinion at the school and pretty swiftly find seven other families at our school who have a child with autism. I'm not one to instigate social occasions, or to harness the power of technology that well either, to be honest, yet I find myself setting up a WhatsApp group for we parents and arranging our first meet up in a pub near the school. I want to call it, 'the club that no one wants to belong to', but decide to settle with 'supporting each other' for now until I get a bit more comfortable.

Our first meet up was at a local pub – six parents who didn't ever want to be meeting with each other at this pub on this Monday night with this objective. The meeting was one of the most positive things I had done since the diagnosis. I met six parents who are facing very similar struggles in their lives. *And they all seem to be ok.* They are having a hard time and we are all facing slightly different struggles, but the most useful part of the evening is to normalise what we are going through. Straight away, I did not feel as alone. There were people out there who understood. There are people out there who have been dealing with this for longer than Steve and I have, and who are going to be able to give us some help. We can learn from their successes and their failures. And they can learn from ours.

One of the dads stunned me with his perspective on autism. He has never, ever shied away from telling his son about what is going on. When they went for the tests, he even said to his son that they were going because they thought he might be autistic and wanted to get it checked out. His child was slightly older than Leo when this was all going on. He can't get his head around why someone might be in denial about it. I make up that the impact on his son must be significantly positive. If the parents hold no shame, if they can completely normalise what is going on for their son, that is bound to pass on to how their son feels about it. This is in contrast to another child's mother who has just told him about his diagnosis after he came home one day from school and asked her if he was autistic. This child has constant one to one support at school so there is a suspicion that one of the other children might have mentioned something. I speak to Steve about how important it is for us to 'control the narrative' with Leo. We decide no shocks and no big reveals. We want this to be something Leo has always known about himself, and yet we are keenly aware that we need to resolve some of our own emotions and thoughts about the diagnosis before we can do this in a neutral way.

The group continues to be a great resource for myself and for the others within it. We have a WhatsApp group in which we share our day to day challenges, learnings and insights with each other. We are trying to meet monthly, socially. The conversation isn't all about autism, but a lot of it is. It's helpful to be able to speak our struggle with people who understand, to be able to share thoughts and ideas, to be able to treat what we are going through as 'normal'. We also realise that, as a group, we are stronger. Not only in our support for one another but also in how we can approach the school, and possibly one day influence beyond the school. There is strength in our numbers. We arranged a meeting with the head teacher of the school and it was clear that he listened to us in a way that perhaps he wouldn't have listened to us as individual parents. At one point, the meeting seemed to lose its way and we meandered. I found myself stepping in and suggesting that we each take it in turns to highlight the experiences of ourselves and of our children at the school. We each stepped in to share with the head teacher how the school has handled our children – the positives and the not so positives. The meeting concluded with a discussion of our 'asks'. Break time can be overwhelming for our children because of their challenges with noise, socialising and unstructured activities. The older children are able to access the library – could an alternative be offered to the younger children too? Could we consider more specialised speech and language therapy, which is more geared to kids on the spectrum? Could any of the support services that we currently access outside of the school be brought in to the school, possibly saving us money as we could guarantee an economy of scale, but moreover to avoid long trips around London after school? I wrote up a summary of the meeting afterwards, in particularly our 'asks', and forwarded it to the head teacher.

Later I reflected on what a positive experience this has been – from setting up the group, to meeting some wonderful parents, through to meeting the head teacher all together. I realised I was stepping into my leadership. I've always spoken about leadership as something that is accessible to anyone, rather than something that is the preserve of people in senior positions. For me, leadership is about recognising the truth of your situation and realising your agency to impact on it. It is about being able to take an honest and hard look, both internally and externally, to see what is really going on, underneath all of our stories and judgements. Armed with that truth, it is understanding what we can do to create a positive impact and make the change that we want to see in our worlds. The opposite of leadership, in my mind, is a victim-like mentality. One in which we perceive things as happening to us, without any understanding of how we can positively create a change.

Don't get me wrong, I've sat in the victim seat many a time. When I was struggling to get pregnant, I couldn't see how anything I did could positively influence the situation I was in. Likewise, when Steve was going through a protracted divorce in the early days of our relationship. When I was working in the media industry, there were times I could act as an agent for change, and equally times when I sat back and felt impotent in making a difference.

The example I always give, to drill the point home that it's not about your seniority, is how the guy sweeping the road could easily step into his leadership. Imagine a car crash happens right in front of him. It's the guy who is able to co-ordinate the request for help and who starts directing the traffic along different routes, all the time maintaining a clear head having worked through his own emotions that might have arisen, that is stepping into his leadership.

In creating this community, not only was I benefiting from the creation of the community, but I was benefitting from the sense that I was making a positive difference to my situation. I was creating something constructive and positive that was supporting myself, my family and the community. For the first time, I was feeling – not that something was happening to me – but that I was creating and conducting something. This feels critical to the concept of resilience; the ability to create impact on what you are going through. I hesitate to call it seizing control, as seizing control can be done from a place of fear and suggests that you are tightly controlling yours and others' behaviours. The difference I think is that leadership comes from a place of positive purpose, rather than fear. For us, that was about wanting to provide support for one another, help make the school a more inclusive environment and to harness the power of the group.

Community and support are also critical functions of resilience. George, Maclean and Craig's work on *Finding Your True North*[49] also talks about the importance of your support section and being purposeful about who you surround yourself with when you are going through critical transitions in your life. They talk about support specifically related to making big, conscious, shifts in your life – such as a major career transition.

Research has also shown how a strong support system can help

49   Maclean, A., George, B. and Craig, N. (2008) *Finding Your True North: A Personal Guide*

people manage the stress of major illnesses, both emotionally and practically. In an interview on Self.com50, Ben Weast, a medical family therapist at the Duke Cancer Center (an American research facility and hospital), says he's often seen this play out in real life. "I've seen this time and time again how having strong support — whatever that looks like—gives these patients a way to process their emotions," he says. "Layers of support that people develop and create around them only help. The specific thing [support systems] provide is hope", Weast says. "It's a very rare human being that can forge ahead and continue at their pace or strength of belief or endurance without other supportive cast for them to lean on, so to speak. In addition to emotional support, other people can help with logistics and practical issues, such as setting up appointments or accompanying you to appointments and providing an 'extra pair of ears'".

At the time of writing, the requirement of support groups within the diversity and inclusion agenda is a topical one. Thus far, one of the ways in which large companies have attempted to create a more inclusive workplace has been in the setting up of specialised groups championing certain sectors of their populations – i.e. women's groups, LGBTQ (Lesbian, Gay, Bisexual, Transgender, Queer) groups and so on. I've often been asked for my point of view on such groups. At my previous employment, one of the first things they did, about ten years ago, was to create a women's group called The Blue Room, and I think the general consensus was that it did more harm than good. It became a focus for many of that group's problems, without finding a way to mobilise change.

More recently, one of the lines of thought has been that we shouldn't be segmenting and separating our work populations along these lines as it's actually just repeating some of the issues

50   https://www.self.com/story/yes-having-a-support-system-really-does-matter-when-youre-battling-a-terminal-illness

of decades previously. If we are telling men that they shouldn't go off on their male-only golf days, surely it's not ok for women to be repeating this by creating women-only spaces. I can also see how it's only by men and women coming together to discuss our gender challenges that real change is going to happen. And yet, I continued to see the advantage of under-represented groups coming together to share and to co-create change.

In the summer of 2017, Deloitte announced a plan to close down its employee affinity groups for women and minorities. Instead, they announced a plan to create inclusion councils where white men would hold important seats at the table. According to Bloomberg[51], after twenty-four years, WIN, the women's initiative at Deloitte, will end. Over the next eighteen months the company will also phase out Globe, which supports gay employees, and groups focused solely on veterans or minority employees. In their place will be so-called inclusion councils that bring together a variety of viewpoints to work on diversity issues. Apparently one of the key motivating factors has been that millennials don't like demographic pigeonholes. I can completely understand the thinking behind this decision, and the need to involve current leadership (which is often white and male) in creating any change, yet I am concerned about what we will miss out on if we lose these spaces for community and support. I'm in agreement with Jennifer Brown (a New York-based inclusion consultant) whom I had the pleasure of meeting at the Emerging Women conference in San Francisco a couple of years ago, and who is also quoted in the article. "We need these groups until such time as people of like identity don't need to close the door and seek a safe space," she says. "We're not there yet."

Indeed, I think if your voice is not the dominant voice in society, or at work, it is easy to think, "Is it just me who thinks like

51   https://www.bloomberg.com/news/articles/2017-07-19/deloitte-thinks-diversity-groups-are-pass

this?" Community can be an important part of resilience in that it will also enable you to find your voice and realise that you are not alone. We are built to connect with other people; our brains are literally wired for it. Community must be important in creating a space for us to tentatively find that voice, express ourselves and build connections with other people. As we do this, we feel less isolated and alone and instead more a part of humanity.

Things you can do to build community when your life is diverted.

1   Set up a support network. If the support you need isn't out there, create it for yourself. Find like-minded people in a similar situation and arrange to meet them regularly. A WhatsApp group is great for quick dissemination of information.

2   Find strength in numbers to co-create change. The lives of those with autism has been immeasurably changed because of the pain and persistence of parents before you. The role of parents cannot be overstated. We know what our children need and are passionate enough about it to really fight for it. Gather a group together and make local suggestions for change – examples might be a quiet area at break time, or an autism-only screening at your local cinema.

3   Be clear on your allies and 'angels'. Some people will drain you of your confidence and energy, while others will support you and make you feel safe. Spend time with the latter group. When others in your network know the challenges your child faces, particularly if you're in public spaces, your 'angels' will step in to help. You may have a special text, emoji or hand signal which just simply says, I need you to step in and be an angel right now.

8

Evolving My Purpose

One of the funny things that happened to Steve and me, when all of this saga kicked off, is that we quickly reverted to gendered stereotypes. Ever since I had set up my consultancy, Steve and I have co-parented. For one year, when Leo was four and Finn was three, we both worked a four-day week. On Mondays, Steve would do the school run with Leo and then stay home with Finn, taking him to his swimming lesson and walking the dog. On Fridays, I would do the school run and then spend the day with Finn. We'd visit friends, go to the park and for a while attended a parenting course together in Stamford Hill, a district of Hackney known for its Hasidic community. Furthermore, Steve and I have both left permanent employment in the media industry to pursue work that is purposeful and meaningful to us. Steve still works flexibly as a consultant at a mobile advertising agency and is also setting up his own running coaching business – The Milestone Pursuit. I set up my own business in 2012, just after Leo was born, when I realised I wanted to support the female career journey as a coach and facilitator. Since then my work has expanded to being about diversity and inclusivity – I described myself in 2012 as on a mission to transform business via the inclusivity of women. Steve and I are both responsible for bringing income into our family, we are both engaged in work that is meaningful to us and we both have a responsibility towards our children. I'm immensely proud of this.

At the beginning, I was concerned that my work on inclusion could be a barrier to Leo getting the support that he needed – in that it was a real blocker for me. I had spent a lot of time by then championing introverts; trying to show people that we live in a world in which extroverts seem to dominate. (S)he who shouts the loudest seems to be the one who is seen as the most intelligent and capable. I am an extrovert (according to the original Myers-Briggs definition, this is about getting my energy externally, from others, rather than internally), who remains interested in the needs of introverts and has even suggested a work stream entitled 'The Introvert Revolution' to one of the agencies with whom I work, inspired by Susan Cain's work[52]. (Susan Cain is an American writer and lecturer who argues that western culture undervalues the traits and capabilities of introverted people, expecting them to adapt to extroverted norms). A friend wondered if my interest in and support of introverts blinded me to the possibility that Leo's social reluctance was down to anything more than introversion.

A couple of weeks after that meeting with the form teacher, we were talking about what we were going to do. Steve said it had become very clear to him that we needed to have a secure income. We couldn't risk having to move home or move schools because we ran out of money. While we were both doing well, our work arrangements certainly ran the risk of being more volatile than most. Steve felt it was his responsibility to 'lean in' at work, get a 'proper' job and ensure our income was fixed and secure for the foreseeable future. I, on the other hand, felt that there needed to be a secure and consistent care provider in the home. Our work arrangements meant

52   Cain, Susan (2013) *Quiet: The Power of Introverts in a World That Can't Stop Talking*

there was a great deal of flexibility in our schedules and the kids might get myself, Steve, my Mum or a masters student (our one day a week child care) picking them up from school each day. I felt sure I would have to quit my work and be more present in the home. We both agreed that we also needed to shore up our relationship with each other. The boys, and especially Leo, were going to need consistency in the long term and a house free from stress. Our relationship had to become a priority.

While this is a fictional example, the mother in the wonderful novel *This is How it Always Is*[53], considers giving up her medical career when her child, born a boy, realises she needs to live as a girl. In *NeuroTribes*[54], Steve Silberman describes how he "learned that it was not unusual for parents whose finances were already strained by the cost of behavioural interventions to have to walk away from careers they loved to effectively become case managers for their children, fielding teams of behavioural therapists while going in to battle with school boards…"

We haven't implemented any of these changes as yet because we realised they were an instinctive reaction to the situation in which we found ourselves, and not necessarily the right thing for our family. It is astonishing how, after all of the work we had put in to find our purpose and then step into that purpose, we might find ourselves in a place of high stress and give that all up. Yes, Leo is going to need consistency, security and a calm(ish) household. Steve and I did not, and do not, need to revert to traditional father and mother roles so as to give that to him. We might still make some changes in our lives. I have had some uncertainties about the school he is at, although he is currently thriving, and we are both unclear as to whether London, with all its hustle and bustle, is the

53   Frankel, Laurie (2017) *This is How it Always Is*

54   Silberman, Steve (2015) *NeuroTribes: The Legacy of Autism and the Future of Neurodiversity*

best place for him to be. However, such changes will be thought through well and through the eyes of everyone in the family.

The thing I keep coming back to is that it is Leo who encouraged me to follow my purpose in the first place. When he was five months old, just looking at him I realised that I couldn't go back to my previous workplace, where I had been heading up big advertising accounts. I also realised that things were really quite tough for women in that industry during my time on maternity leave with Leo, partly because of my experiences when pregnant and while away from the office with him. I thought that if I was going to leave Leo so as to go to work, it had to be to do work that was meaningful to me. Steve was still working full-time in a managing director role back then, and so I was lucky enough to be able to take a bit of a risk. I had already trained as a coach when aiming for management in the media agency that I worked at, and realised that I could use these coaching qualifications to support women in the workplace. The media industry, like many industries, doesn't have a problem recruiting women at the bottom of the ladder. Instead, the problem lies in retaining and promoting these women – especially as they move through their thirties. Here two struggles emerge. Women might struggle navigating maternity leave and family with the demands on the workplace and also this coincides with a time when many women are finding it hard to move from management into leadership positions. I set up a coaching business offering interventions at these two inflection points in the form of maternity coaching and female leadership coaching.

I then pretty swiftly came to two further realisations. Firstly, I was sending the message that the women needed fixing. This is clearly not true. With two boys by this time, I was horrified by the high male suicide rate in our country and soon began to realise that masculinity was having a crisis of its own. I started the #HeANDShe conference because I wanted men and women to come together to talk about some of our gender challenges, rather than separating into non-gender-diverse groups. In fact, the challenges facing men were simply the other side of the same coin as the challenges facing women. We are all caught up in these stereotyped views of how we should be thinking, feeling and behaving – and it's not working for any of us.

My second realisation was that just focusing on women, or even gender, is the antithesis of inclusivity. There are so many people who, for so many reasons, feel that they can't show up as themselves in the workplace. Our unconscious bias gets in the way from the moment a CV arrives, making it harder for Muslims, people of colour, those with disabilities, older people and many more to get taken as seriously as white, middle-class men in the workplace. Once in the workplace, as already mentioned, introverts get asked to adapt to the predominant culture – which is often extrovert. They are asked to cope with open plan offices, attend brainstorm meetings and told to 'speak up' more. I realised with Leo early on that I was raising an introverted child and, inspired by Susan Cain, became interested in how I could celebrate his introversion, rather than seeing it as something to be 'fixed', along with applying learnings to the workplace.

The work that I did began to evolve. Rather than just focus on women, I started to ask how organisations could better support everyone to show up as themselves and be valued for it. Instead of championing the inclusivity of women, I suggested businesses could be transformed via inclusivity. Period. I offered consultancy and training courses aimed at helping organisations to understand the business case for diversity and inclusivity, to discover where their own 'unconscious biases' might lie and to start holding themselves accountable for behaving in a more inclusive manner.

Last year, and still before the first mention of the A word, I sat outside on a scorching London summer day talking to a friend of mine, Lauren Burton, who is also a coach and the founder of a successful coaching business called 'L_eap'. I was talking about the difficulties I was experiencing in juggling work and family. I complained that I kept getting drawn back to my family and it meant I wasn't investing as much timewise as others were in their businesses, and consequently my business wasn't being as successful. As well as reminding me to stop listening to the comparison gremlin, Lauren gave me some advice that has stayed with me ever since. She said, "The thing is Rox, your family means the world to you. Your purpose in life is bound up with your family, as well as your work, otherwise you wouldn't keep getting drawn back to your family. Do you think mums who are also female war photographers are always drawn back? They're not. Their purpose is in their work, and that's fine. That's why they leave their family for months to pursue their purpose. Your purpose is bound up with your family, and your work. You need to align the two." It was an astonishing moment as I realised that my purpose was, and remains, "to support people to show up as themselves". Whether I am at home with the boys or at work, I can align myself to this purpose and try my best to honour it all the time.

I rang Lauren in those difficult months running up to Christmas and thanked her again for her wisdom. She didn't realise just how much comfort her words had given me, and how much direction too. Now we were talking about a possible autism diagnosis for Leo, it became really clear for me that I needed to support Leo to show up as himself. For me, this isn't about expecting Leo to behave differently. Leo will behave how he wants to behave. My role is to create the environment so that he can show up as himself (by reducing stress and pressure for example) and championing his authentic self in the environments where they try and get a square peg in a round hole (such as school). Lauren and I were both in tears as I thanked her for her time and wisdom. I wanted to be sure to tell her what an impact she had made on my life.

A couple of weeks after the diagnosis, the topic of neurodiversity started to come up in my training sessions. At this stage, my understanding of this is that we were talking about how people with neurological differences such as autism can work alongside those that are more neurotypical. I was told at one company, that I had just begun working for, about the challenges they had with someone who was on the autism spectrum who was working in a client-facing role. Before learning of his diagnosis, they had not been understanding about his difficulties in communicating with clients and had started a disciplinary procedure. He told them about his autism and, this was music to my ears at the time, sat down with him to work out how they could better support him in the workplace. He was moved to a non-client-facing role in which his tasks were more about problem solving, rather than client development. Unfortunately, there's no 'happy ending' to the story and the employee ended up leaving anyway so we don't know how he's doing now. I'm told he found their efforts quite difficult to 'accept', feeling he was being given special treatment that he didn't deserve.

I realised early on that diversity and inclusivity of course extends to those with autism, with a slight feeling of shame that this hadn't occurred to me until the situation had become personal. The unemployment rate is shockingly high (only 16% of those diagnosed are in full-time employment once they reach adulthood[55]) and yet many of these people have so much to offer to the modern workplace. Companies are looking for support in how to achieve diversity and I want to be part of the solution. I can't

55   http://www.autism.org.uk/about/what-is/myths-facts-stats.aspx

change my son, but I can help create a world that is more tolerant of him and that meets his needs. Hell, I can try and create a world that sees his difference as his superpower.

Scrolling through Twitter one day I came across the story of a tech firm in the US which has gone further and is championing the business benefits that employing those on the autism spectrum can bring[56]. The article talks of autism being a feature rather than a bug in the workplace and describes the difference in business results that the company has achieved. The company gives some very clear actions that can be taken so as to accommodate those on the spectrum. Firstly, they suggest getting rid of interviews. Even outside of the topic of autism, research has shown that the interview process is riddled with bias with leaders choosing people who they connect with and who, typically, think or look like them. Instead of interviews, which would come with the barrier of having to connect emotionally with the interviewer, this company has championed problem solving as part of the recruitment process and also looked for behavioural traits such as coachability and perseverance. Furthermore, they have implemented rules – such as, emails can't be more than seven sentences long and must be reported to a supervisor if the trail goes on for more than two back-and-forth exchanges. The thinking being that there might be a hidden issue, which can't be spotted by someone taking the email more on face value. Also, workers are able to keep their faces hidden on teleconferences should they wish.

A couple of weeks later, I was invited to speak at a BIMA diversity meeting (British Interactive Media Association). BIMA is Britain's digital community, aiming to drive excellence and innovation across the digital industry. I arrived before my slot, but after the start of the meeting, to hear Nadya Powell, co-founder of Utopia (and head of the diversity council at BIMA), giving a great

---

56   https://medium.com/neodotlife/ultra-testing-433b9a32a521

introduction to the importance of diversity in the industry. I was nodding along and saw her diversity statistics slide and realised that there was no mention of neurodiversity. I spoke up and asked if this could perhaps be considered as part of conversations about diversity in the digital industry going forwards. The response was fantastic, once people understood what I was talking about. Many people in the room simply did not know what neurodiversity is, and equally my husband didn't understand fully when I got home and was excited about managing to speak in the meeting. John Elder Robinson, in 'Psychology Today'[57], writes, "To me, neurodiversity is the idea that neurological differences like autism and ADHD are the result of normal, natural variation in the human genome. This represents a new and fundamentally different way of looking at conditions that were traditionally pathologized; it's a viewpoint that is not universally accepted though it is increasingly supported by science." I read this and for the first time felt like I was reading something that reflected my own thoughts.

Rather than represent autism as a disorder, there are people out there who believe it is a normal variation in how humans are made up. What if there is nothing 'wrong' with Leo at all? What is 'wrong' is that the world is not set up to cater for that difference in the human genome. We are ignorant as to what people with autism need so as to be safe and to survive and thrive in our modern world. The National Autistic Society's latest campaign – Too Much Information – is a great piece of communication aimed at reducing that ignorance and explaining why those with autism can struggle so much with modern life.

I decided it was time to start speaking to a wider audience about my thinking and experiences, and sent the following out to my email database:

---

57   https://www.psychologytoday.com/blog/my-life-aspergers/201310/what-is-neurodiversity

Neurodiversity starts at home

"Neurodiversity may be every bit as crucial for the human race as biodiversity is for life in general. Who can say what form of wiring will prove best at any given moment?" Harvey Blume[58].

"Neurodiversity is an essential form of human diversity. The idea that there is one 'normal' or 'healthy' type of brain or mind or one 'right' style of neurocognitive functioning, is no more valid than the idea that there is one 'normal' or 'right' gender, race or culture." Nick Walker[59].

Hi

In the spring of this year, one of my children was diagnosed with High Functioning Autism. It has been a challenging time for our family and I'm sure the challenges will continue for some time yet. However, we're definitely on the rising side of the change curve now – beginning to see the gifts and learnings in our situation.

Why I'm writing about it today is because it has really shifted my thinking about the work that The Hobbs Consultancy does.

Firstly, I have been so relieved to have been my own boss during this period so that I can take time out and rest when I have needed to. I simply would not have been able to process the very strong and challenging emotions that came up for me while working flat out. I applaud the introduction of 'mental health days' and bosses that welcome them. I can truly see, from my own experience, why, on some days, my focus was best spent at home processing my thoughts and feelings, rather than trying to muddle through at work. In addition to this, it occurs to me that there is a need for boundaries too when we're talking about showing up authentically. Authenticity isn't about blurting the first thing on your mind. It would simply not have been appropriate for me to have been downloading my feelings about this to you all five months

58   Blume, Harvey (1998) 'Neurodiversity: On the neurological underpinnings of geekdom', The Atlantic; https://www.theatlantic.com/magazine/archive/ 1998/09/neurodiversity/305909/

59   https://www.identityfirstautistic.org/the-neurodiversity-paradigm-

ago as I was working through some dark times. We want to show up as ourselves in the workplace and an important function of that is to know your own boundaries – put simply, what's ok and what's not ok for you. For me, one of those lines is not to share personal matters to a broad audience until we've processed them.

The other big insight for me is that I have spent the past five years championing diversity and inclusion in the workplace, and haven't mentioned neurodiversity until this became a relevant topic for my family. I have since introduced the topic at the BIMA council and at various tech agencies! As I explored the topic of autism in the workplace, I came across a company called Ultra Testing who test new websites for bugs. What makes Ultra Testing different is that most of its testers are on the autism spectrum. And the thinking behind this is not an altruistic one, but a business one – simply put, they believe the tendency of some people with autism to obsessively focus on detail gives them a distinct competitive advantage. Here are just some of the tweaks they made to their company culture so as to accommodate autism:

- They rethought the hiring process. Interviews can be a barrier for individuals on the spectrum and there is much evidence to show they are riddled with bias anyway. Rather than interviews, theyused questionnaires, essays and tests.
- They codified the rules and expectations of people to an unusual degree
- Employees typically work remotely and communicate over email or Slack[60] (this gives them time to process the information with a lag).
- They are tolerant of spelling mistakes (autism and dyslexia often go hand in hand)
- Emails have to be less than 700 characters long and if the

---

60   A cloud-based set of team collaboration tools and services founded by Stewart Butterfield

back and forth exchange goes on more than twice, employ-ees are instructed to tell a supervisor (the thought being there's probably an underlying issue that the employee isn't picking up on).

As well as giving me hope for the future employability of my son, this case study really has shown me the small tweaks we can make in a corporate culture that enable people to show up as themselves. In this case, those on the spectrum need a different way to get through the door. This has been followed by some explicit changes to 'how we do things around here' (a great definition of culture) so that they can not only show up as themselves but also thrive. I'm sure the advertising, tech and creative industries can learn a lot from this one small success story.

Neurodiversity is "the diversity of human brains and minds – the infinite variation in neurocognitive functioning within our species." We are all neurodiverse, it is the nature of human individuality. The neuro-diversity paradigm is a specific perspective on neurodiversity respect-ing the natural diversity of minds and the variability of functioning and how this can, when embraced, act as a source of creative potential. The neurodiversity movement celebrates the differences and unique abilities exhibited by people with autism, pursuing equality, respect, and full soci-etal inclusion for the neurodivergent (having a brain that functions in ways that diverge significantly from societal 'normal' standards).

In essence, difference in brain functionality is innate, not to be pathologised and forms an important part of the diversity agenda. Our differences can be our superpowers and yet society can use it to stereotype and create "otherness". At The Hobbs Consultancy we are committed to talking about this alongside other axes of difference.

With love,

Rox

It was the most opened, commented upon and replied to email that I have ever sent out. People appreciated the honesty and authenticity of the communication.

"I was really touched and inspired by you when I read this Roxanne. These are the conversations the world needs to be having."

"Such an honest and brave e-mail. Thanks. Definitely think we need to integrate neurodiversity into the next British Diversity Experiment and clearly a lot I need to learn."

"I just wanted to respond to this personal email by saying how much I respect your authenticity in the manner with which you share about your child. Brave and courageous communication that moves me."

What have I learnt about resilience during this time period? It's easy to lose sight of your purpose and your own path when things are challenging at home with your children. We can fall quickly into giving everything up, and that might well be right for some families. I think being clear on the change you want to make in the world is critical. It is also hard to balance what your children need and to follow your own path. I am hugely fortunate in a way – my purpose and what is required of me at home are congruent. They are moving in the same direction. I also learnt that you can't incorporate something that is so emotionally challenging into your work until you have done your own work. What I mean is that there are a lot of people out there in the world fighting for change. When that fight has emotional weight behind it, it can certainly create the passion to fight harder and stronger. However, it also makes it harder for you to keep a clear head and maintain your focus. I wanted to be sharing and pursuing change having processed the feelings that were coming up for me.

How you can evolve your purpose when your life is diverted.

1   Don't make long-term decisions in the midst of despair. You may end up wanting to make big changes in how you live your life, as a result of your life's changed direction. However, don't rush into these. At the beginning, make short-term adaptations, which create time to process what is happening. Once you start to emerge from that initial overwhelm, you can consider the longer term.

2   Consider your 'purpose' – the reason why you are here and the difference you want to make. Having coached a lot of women through difficult situations, I have always been struck by how frequently the 'lowest low' becomes the cause, which you want to contribute to in the world. The good news is that you are well placed to help make this change because of your experience. What is it about your life's diversion that you think you can help those around you with? Start with baby steps – we're not talking about changing careers here (at least not at the beginning!). Your baby step might be one other person you can help or one change you want to see happen in your local school or community.

3   Stay honest. Keep it real. A heartfelt plea from me on this one. The neurotypical community, and on a broader scale those whose lives haven't been diverted (yet), would benefit hugely from hearing our truth. People want to see real. It builds connection. It also gives others permission for their messy feelings when the time comes. And, when people understand, they can stop being scared, start to contribute to change and help us remove the stigma.

9

Appreciating Our Common Humanity

"What surprises me time and time again as I travel around the constituency is that we are far more united and have far more in common with each other than things that divide us"[61], said Jo Cox at her now famous maiden speech to parliament. Jo, who died after being shot and stabbed multiple times in the summer of 2016 by a neo-Nazi, on her way to a constituency surgery, used her speech to address and champion the benefits of immigration. A part of her legacy has been the continued spreading of this message by her inspiring husband Brendan Cox. Coincidentally, on the day of writing this, the heroic miner, Bernard Kenny, who tried to stop her murder, also died, aged 79[62] – so it feels right to mention his act of courage too.

While Jo Cox was specifically talking about immigration, and was killed against the ugly backdrop of the EU referendum in the UK, the message resonates on multiple levels. I have used it when talking about gender at my #HeANDShe conference. Our very first conference was held in the summer of 2016 and had the intention of bringing men and women together to talk

---

61   http://www.huffingtonpost.co.uk/entry/jo-cox-maiden-speech_uk_5762de5be4b03f24e3db840f

62   http://news.sky.com/story/ex-miner-bernard-kenny-who-tried-to-stop-jo-cox-murder-dies-aged-79-10989046

about gender. I was hugely inspired by the work of Cordelia Fine[63] who argues convincingly that gender is a cultural construct. It is both fluid and not binary. I wanted to start a conversation about what could be possible if we could escape those binary expectations we have created around what it is to be female and what it is to be male. I wanted to tell the advertising industry that they, as creators of culture, shape these perceptions. I asked, "What if we could come together and create a system in which everyone can be themselves?" I asked, "What if our humanity was our defining characteristic, rather than our femininity or masculinity?" The following summer, I asked myself the same question with regards to autism.

In the summer of 2017, I was lucky enough to take an extended holiday to Bali. With money left to me by my Grandma Totty as inheritance, I booked all four of us flights and an Airb'n'b villa in Seminyak for a month. I love travel and the past couple of summers we've all been to the United States where Steve can work in San Francisco and I get to hang out in a new city with the boys. This year, I was having a strop about Donald Trump when we came to booking our summer holiday and decided to head in the opposite direction. I felt like we'd had a tough time of it and that some time together as a family would be beneficial for all of us. I also really wanted to spend some more time writing, and thought that being away from London and work would give me some headspace. So as to achieve that, I booked a local nanny to take care of the kids in the mornings so that I could write and Steve could work. I was also advised to book a driver, rather than hire a car, as the traffic in Bali is pretty gnarly and there are limited maps and road signs. Shortly after we booked, my Mum – whom the boys call Nana Cherry – decided she would like to come along too.

63   Fine, Cordelia (2010) *Delusions of Gender*

I wrote each day in a beautiful little restaurant called Nook. It's on the edge of Seminyak and is completely open to paddy fields on two of its sides. The inside is decorated with distressed wooden furniture, huge amounts of foliage and there's beautiful, gentle music playing in the background. I could feel the soft breeze coming in through the open sides to the restaurant and saw local people working in the paddy fields. I drank iced coffee and ate 'Nook Pancakes' – pancakes cooked with pineapple inside of them. I sat there, having ordered the same items off the menu, and writing, every week day at 9am for much of our trip. In the afternoon, I would head back to the villa at midday, have lunch with the family and then take the boys out swimming somewhere for the afternoon. Around 4pm, we would head down to the beach where Steve would join us and we'd go to our favourite beach bar for beers at sunset, and have dinner there. Once it got completely dark, at just before 7pm, we tended to walk back off the beach, cut through the W hotel as it provided the quickest route back to our villa, and began the boys' bedtime routine of showers and stories.

When we arrived, I didn't feel quite so relaxed, peaceful or at home. The seventeen-hour journey consisted of two flights and an extremely short turnaround in Qatar. We arrived exhausted at the villa at 1.30am and had a brief moment of joy when the boys jumped naked into the swimming pool. The next morning, we all managed to sleep until about 11am when we woke up, exhausted and disorientated. The villa owner showed up to make sure we had everything we need. Then the driver showed up asking where we wanted to go that day. Finally, a tour operator showed up asking which trips we wanted to book. I couldn't answer any of their questions, I barely knew what day it was and my brain was just not working. Too many questions and my brain just seemed unable to engage. Soon these three were joined by a nanny, a cleaner and the 'pool guy'. Everyone was asking things of us and we sat there, mutely, unable to answer and unable to think straight.

Later on, still bleary-eyed, we ventured out to Seminyak to buy some groceries. There was absolute traffic chaos. The roads in Bali are not wide enough for the sheer volume of traffic, there are limited traffic lights and roads have a tendency to be shut down with no notice because of a local ceremony. We were starving and couldn't seem to get to a supermarket because the traffic wasn't moving. When we finally got to one, we couldn't find the food we needed and also couldn't make sense of the money (GBP£1 is about IDR17,000 so the numbers get very large and confusing very quickly). People kept asking us if we needed taxis or massages. It was absolutely overwhelming – the humidity, the traffic noise, the general busy-ness. My brain responded to this by shutting down almost. I could feel myself going in on myself and pulling back from everyone around me. Even if I had wanted to engage fully with someone, I wouldn't have been able to.

I struggled to adjust for a good week to ten days at the start of our trip. Bali is seven hours ahead of the UK and so the jet lag is harsh on the system. The first few nights, both Steve and I woke up around 1am and didn't get back sleep again until about 5am. We then got woken up at around 8am by the boys. Just as we got in to our sleep rhythm, Leo woke up at 1am and was awake for four hours. We were absolutely shattered, leaving the calm of the villa felt like an assault to the senses and, in order to do anything, we needed to give instructions in advance to a driver who we were struggling to communicate with.

I started to wonder if this is what life feels like to Leo all the time. Actually, Leo and Finn adapted much quicker than Steve and I. They took it much more in their stride, while Steve and I were still floundering. It all felt just *too much*. So many people were asking me questions and I simply found myself unable to answer any of them. I could feel myself going in on myself, bringing the shutters down and almost stopping communicating apart from the absolute necessities. I was reminded of the National Autistic Society's campaign, Too Much Information. The information on their website begins, "I am autistic and sometimes I get too much information. It's like everything's building up inside my head. Like my brain is crowded with questions – and about to explode. I try my hardest to filter it all. But there's too much, and saying anything is too hard."[64]

I wondered if this mind-destroying jet lag, coupled with the assault on the senses of a different place and culture, along with the incessant questions of my family and also those trying to help us or sell us things, was the best way I will ever experience what is going on in Leo's brain. I have no better way of describing it, than to say it felt like *too much*. And that my response to it was, firstly, to shut down and isolate myself. My second response, after a period of adjustment, was to find solace in the things that I knew. The restaurant I returned to morning after morning, the items on the menu that I recognised and enjoyed. We developed patterns – we worked in the mornings, played together in the afternoons, ate together at the beach in the early evening. We asked the nanny and the driver to arrive at the same times day after day, as it meant we knew what we were doing and could follow our routines. We even brought some semblance of our UK working patterns over with us. Weekdays were for 'working', weekends were for taking longer road trips.

Hilariously, it was Leo, one day, who called us out on our rigid routines. "Mama", he complained, "you are always making us go to the beach in the afternoons. You are always making us

64   http://www.autism.org.uk/get-involved/tmi.aspx

watch the sunset and have dinner at the beach. Every day! You are such a bad Mama!" Such a tough life, Leo, living in a villa in Bali! Truth be told, these routines provided us with scaffolding when we were feeling unsettled, and possibly even anxious. It was a way of minimising the questions and supporting us in feeling secure. Just like Kanner identified, we coped with 'too much' by wanting to self-isolate (he called it *extreme autistic aloneness)* and by creating our own routines (*an anxiously obsessive desire for the maintenance of sameness* which he theorised was born out of a deep-seated anxiety which could only be kept at bay by maintaining sameness[65]).

I think the first step to breaking down the stigma around autism has to be to look inside ourselves. Indeed, Kristin Neff[66] says that compassion involves "recognising our shared human condition, flawed and fragile as it is". Up until now, my manifestation of our common humanity had been to look towards all of the other mothers in the world facing challenges rearing their children. How could I look at autism through the lens of our common humanity? Asperger himself thought that the autism he was seeing in Vienna was "not at all rare"[67] and had a broad range of manifestations – from the child who couldn't speak, to the child who had the ability to focus on one subject intensely and for a prolonged period. Silberman points out, "In other words, it was a spectrum. Once you knew what to look for, you saw it everywhere"[68]. I would suggest that we all, at same time in our lives, experience anxiety. We all have our coping mechanisms. For many, those coping mechanisms may well be a tendency to go quiet, even if only in certain circumstances. Also, we are all typically creatures of some kind of habit – using our routines to create order and structure in

65   As quoted by Steve Silberman (2015) in *NeuroTribes: The Legacy of Autism and the Future of Neurodiversity*

66   Neff, Kirstin (2011) *Self Compassion*. This quote is on her Facebook page – https://www.facebook.com/selfcompassion/

67   Asperger, Hans as quoted in Silberman, Steve (2015) *NeuroTribes: The Legacy of Autism and the Future of Neurodiversity*

68   Ibid

our lives. As a training consultant in organisations, I notice every year that my bookings hike significantly in September and I can only hypothesise that the 'back to school feeling' of September, hardwired in to our brains from our early years, lasts a lifetime.

During the time I was in Bali, reading and writing about the history of autism, including the murder of disabled children along with Jews in Nazi Germany, there was a resurgence of the far right in the US. In Charlottesville, Virginia, there was a white nationalist rally one Saturday – organised in opposition to a plan to remove a statue of Robert E. Lee, commander of the Confederate States army in the American Civil War. During this march, a car ploughed in to a group of counter protesters, killing Heather Heyer, a 32-year-old paralegal who was a passionate advocate of the disenfranchised. In the New York Times, I read that people in the US and beyond "were grappling with the blatant display of attitudes that many believed had been buried, but the extremists who rallied were newly energized and planning their next moves"[69]. While police departments across the country were bracing for what they feared could be similar events, Donald Trump offered an evasive condemnation of the white supremacists.

Many commentators in the States are beginning to talk about how the country needs to 'own' its history of white supremacy so as to heal from it. The morning I was writing, in Bali in August, Brené Brown held a Facebook live event[70] in which she addressed the events of Charlottesville and said that collectively we need to own our stories. Her Rising Strong work is about owning our individual stories so that we can write the endings of them – just as I have delved into and 'owned' the difficult feelings of grief and shame that arose at the beginning of this process, and stared down the unconscious stories

---

69   https://www.nytimes.com/2017/08/13/us/charlottesville-virginia-overview.html

70   https://www.facebook.com/brenebrown/

that were arising at the same time. In the same way, she suggests, we need to own our macro stories so that we can, together, write our own endings. It is looking at resilience through a macro lens. How do we, as the human race, heal from our past and adapt to change?

Drawing parallels with the autism story, we certainly have a painful history from which we need to collectively heal. Even before the terrible events of the 1930s and 1940s, people in our history who have been seen as 'different' or 'other' have been shamefully treated. Women were burnt at the stake, gay men were castrated, disabled children were chained to beds in institutions. I can hardly bring myself to write about it. And yet that is the point. We need to tell these stories so that we can write our own endings. I cannot write the story of the child with autism – that is Leo's story to tell, and the story of all of the other wonderful children who have been diagnosed with autism. But I can tell the parent's story and reflect on how history has treated the parent and how we might still be healing from that history. Unless we speak to it, that energy (that story, if you like) is still out there, influencing our thoughts, feelings and behaviours. Speaking to it allows us to heal and then, rather than getting stuck in our fear, allows us to ask, "if not like that, then how?"

How do we want to treat those who are 'atypical' within our society? At the moment, a lot of energy is being spent on supporting them to 'fit in'. In some ways, this is just another manifestation of the paradigm in which we were trying to 'cure' people of their autism. Parents, under the advice of the medical community, have, in the past, tried electric shock therapy (electrocute solitary twins often enough and they can be taught to hug their parents)[71], punishment-based behavioural therapies and extreme diets, to name just a few of the attempts to cure their children of their autism. It seems to be that we now invest energy in occupational therapy and speech and

71   http://www.newstatesman.com/politics/health/2015/09/beautiful-minds-sometimes-brutal-history-treating-autism

language therapy, often with the desire that the children are more 'normal'. I'm aware that there is an important line to tread here. Surely, as parents, ultimately it is independence for our child that is one of our overarching aims. Obviously if children need support to learn how to, say, prepare food for themselves, that can be seen as a positive intervention. My push back is that, in my experience so far, some of these interventions seem to have the ambition of meeting a normal developmental timeline at their heart. A fear of the child developing at his/her different rate seems more the driver, than perhaps the long-term desires for children to be happy, confident and, ultimately, independent.

I wonder how much the so-called Autism Wars are also related. In the 1998, the medic Andrew Wakefield wrote a now discredited article in The Lancet linking autism with the MMR vaccine. That article has become one of the most discredited and refuted articles in recent history, and there is now clear evidence that some of the data was falsified[72]. The charismatic Wakefield, understandably, enthralled parents with his theory. I can understand how compelling it would be to blame the pharmaceutical industry, particularly after psychologists such as Kanner and Bettelheim had blamed parents for years. Added to which, finding a 'villain', that can be stopped, also implies that one day there is hope for an end to autism. All the while this was going on, Lorna Wing[73] was tirelessly campaigning to have the diagnostic criteria expanded so that the children who most needed it could be sure of getting help on the NHS. She was quietly telling everyone that the increase in the number of cases (between 1990 and 2000 the number of cases of autism in the UK registered for disability payments with the Family Fund increased 22% a year[74])

72 http://www.bmj.com/content/342/bmj.c7452

73 http://www.telegraph.co.uk/news/obituaries/10886838/Lorna-Wing-obituary.html

74 http://www.newstatesman.com/politics/health/2015/09/beautiful-minds -sometimes-brutal-history-treating-autism

was because the diagnostic criteria had widened and more people were seeking help. Forgive me, but I cannot help but see this as yet another example of a charismatic male being listened to over and above a quiet and hard-working female.

I am not for one minute underestimating the challenge that raising a child with autistic characteristics creates for many families. I am, however, fighting for a wider acceptance of difference. I think we need to look within ourselves as to why we, on an individual level, have such a strong reaction to it. I think we need to look at our history to understand, on a societal level, why we want people to conform and to fit in. Times are a-changing. The modern world is perhaps the perfect stage for those with autistic characteristics to make a huge difference. Certain traits – the obsessive interests, an affinity for rules and patterns, and close focus – might be useful skills in the digital age. It might be time to view the rise in the rates of autism not as a problem, but as a gift. This may well be our next frontier. Just as one of the stories of the twenty-first century has been about opposing the diminishment of the female and the feminine, the potential is there for a revolution in how we think about 'neurodiversity'.

What you can do to appreciate our common humanity when your life is diverted.

1   Let go of timelines. Whether it be a timeline for your own 'recovery' or your child's development, don't obsess over how long something '*should*' take. It will take as long as it takes. This is not the same as saying don't get support if you are concerned that you are stuck somewhere. More not to let somebody's idea of a normal timeline become a stick with which to beat yourself.

2   Be curious. Pay attention to how you act when you are under extreme stress. What are your go-to coping strategies? What do you have in common with your partner, your friend and your child? Rather than looking for difference, be curious about what it is that we have in common.

3   Tell your story. The world needs to hear your voice. The discredited voices of the medical community of 1960s and of the 1990s still get too much airtime and have a disproportionate impact on our collective sense of what autism is. We need to embolden parents' voices, hear their stories and how they fight for and champion their children. More than that, we need to hear the voices of those actually with autism. We need to be asking people with autism what their lives are like and what they need so that, finally, they can be fully involved in shaping their future.

10

Understanding Resilience

As autumn slowly arrives in London, I am aware that it is a year since this story started. The changing of the season causes me to reflect on the changes that have happened to our family in the past year. A year ago, we were free of the cloud of anxiety that currently sits over us. In so many ways, we have moved together through our difficult emotions and learnt so much about ourselves and our family. And yet, we still get knocked over. Of course, we do.

So often, I see 'resilience' being used as a stick to beat people with. We expect people to be able to pick themselves up again from the struggles, the pains, even the horrors, of their lives. I hear my colleague, Lisa, berating herself on a supervision call. She has moved her family from Brighton to Bristol because of her husband's work and is struggling with the adjustment. So much so, she has a viral infection that she just can't seem to shake. I hear her saying, "I should be better than this, I should have adjusted by now", and wonder what it is within us that believes we should be able to adjust to transporting our whole lives from one place to another without pain or struggle. It makes sense to me that it would take her a good few months to start to adjust to such a change. And yet, it is hard for me to extend the same generosity to myself or my husband. The whole interest in resilience in the workplace could easily add to this sense of pressure; that we should be being more resilient and therefore getting back to our best, productive selves as quickly as possible.

I'm not going to sit here and write that after a year of facing my emotions and stories I have transcended our struggle and have returned to a perfect and happy existence. What is true is that I have moments of joy and of clarity about my family, and I have moments of struggle. I have moments in which I can step into my leadership and visualise a world in which we can ensure those who aren't neurotypical are included, welcomed and celebrated for their difference. And then bring people along with me on that journey. I also have days where I cry salty tears of frustration that I cannot communicate well with my son in his anger. Today I have bruises all over my legs where he has kicked me out of frustration at his family and the world.

I'm beginning to reframe resilience as a process. It's a process which we have to go through, whenever anything hard happens, which involves staring into and experiencing our pain. When I heard Brené Brown speak in Texas, she said over and over, "We cannot deny our pain." To say, "some people are more resilient than others" to me speaks of comparison, of a standard to which we must reach and a pressure for us to not feel our pain. Genuinely, I believe that many of the problems the world is currently facing are as a result of us trying to avoid being with our pain. For us to go out into the world and lead, to champion change, necessitates us having worked through a lot of our emotions and being really clear about our driving forces. This takes as long as it takes. Where the driving force is our pain, I think we are going to see increased suffering, anger and conflict. Let me give you some examples.

A good friend of mine, Iain, spoke at my recent #HeANDShe conference about abortion. I was terrified about him speaking because I had never heard abortion discussed in a non-emotive way. Maybe non-emotive is perhaps the wrong choice of words. I had never heard abortion discussed without anger, judgement and a binary pro-choice/pro-life distinction. His talk was beautiful. He spoke about what it was like, as a man who dearly wanted his girlfriend to progress with their pregnancy, to experience the termination of that pregnancy. He had worked through his emotions at such a deep level that he spoke without anger, without judgement and, perhaps most importantly, without making anybody in that room wrong for the choices or beliefs that they might have. He modelled vulnerability as he shared his struggle and also his desire for a higher-level conversation around abortion. Something magic happened in that room which could not have happened if he hadn't 'done his own work'.

Harvey Weinstein is in the news. He stands accused of the rape and sexual harassment of many, many women. The collective trauma around this is evident to me. Most women will have, at some stage, been sexually assaulted. For these women, myself included, reading the stories and listening to the audiotapes is triggering in itself. I don't think we can have a conversation about how to change the system when we are speaking from this place of pain. I see a collective anger at men, a desire to control their behaviour and an understandable desire to be heard, having not been heard for years. And I'm not sure we can create sustainable change from that place. It is the system that needs to change. We live in a system in which people's reports of assaults are not listened to and we are all a part of that system. It's not going to change when we are in that place of blame, judgement and pain avoidance.

This autumn, I also returned to Courage Camp in Texas, which is where I heard Kristin Neff speak eighteen months ago about self-compassion (and practically had to be carried out of the room). It feels like another full circle. There's a group of people here who don't know about what has happened to me over the past eighteen months and they, as expected, ask, "Hey, Rox. What's new? What's changed?" I realise I don't want this story to be the one that defines me yet I also want to own it rather than deny it. I notice the twinge I feel when I tell my dear colleague Debbie, who previously has been so vocal about how adorable my "little munchkins" are, and wonder if she'll feel the same adoration of them as she did before. I'm walking a line with these people in which I want to be honest about my struggle, but also I know this isn't the only story of the last year. My business is doing fantastically; I've spent some wonderful time in Bali and have had many fun moments with every member of my family.

My consulting business, The Hobbs Consultancy, has started speaking about neurodiversity. I partnered last month with Ali Hanan from Creative Equals to host a Neurodiversity breakfast. As far as I'm aware, it was the first event of its kind in the advertising industry in London. It was truly a peak experience for me – a moment in which I knew I was exactly where I should be. It kicked off with Sam Phillips, chief marketing officer for Omnicom Media Group, talking about her family situation (her eldest son has Down syndrome among other challenges).

Emotionally, for both herself and me, she read the poem that inspired the title for this book – 'Diverted to Holland'. This renowned poem by Emily Perl Kingsley is about having a child with a disability. The poem describes being on a flight to Italy, when you find out that you are being diverted to Holland. Its message is that, while you haven't ended up where you planned to be, Holland isn't that bad once you stop to appreciate the view. The poem has been adopted by the autism community and is given by many organisations to new parents of children with special needs issues. A response essay describing the impact on families of raising a child with severe autism was later created titled, "Welcome to Beirut" – referencing the suffering of the Lebanese civil war.

After Sam had read 'Diverted to Holland', a speaker from Project Search talked about how the company places and mentors those on the spectrum in the workplace, and she shared some of their successes. I facilitated a workshop about what difference people want to see in our industry and the obstacles that might be in the way. It was a very hard and very fulfilling morning. I was full of emotion – but it wasn't anger or pain. I think it was resonance. That I was exactly where I was supposed to be and trying to make a positive contribution to the world around me.

We're now in the midst of planning a day event for next March called #DiverseMinds and, as the curator of its content, I am having extraordinary and fascinating conversations with people on the front line; people who are trying to change workplace culture to make it more accommodating of neurodiversity. I speak to Ray Coyle at Auticon which only recruit people on the autism spectrum and "are passionate about how autistic talent can enhance your business". Auticon promote the strengths of those on the spectrum and say that, while the strengths are highly individualistic, they frequently include:

- distinctive logical and analytical abilities
- sustained concentration and perseverance even when tasks are repetitive
- conscientiousness, loyalty and sincerity
- an exceptional eye for details, deviations and potential errors
- continuously thorough target/actual comparisons and a genuine awareness for quality

- a strong interest in factual matters and comprehensive technical expertise.[75]

I speak to Nadya Powell, co-founder of Utopia (a platform aimed at re-wiring business for the age of creativity), who tells me of a female advertising creative that she has worked with. "She is a brilliant and creative lady who thinks so differently. From my perspective neurodiverse people bring brilliance and the onus is on people such as myself, who are not on any spectrums, to find ways of ensuring we don't smother this brilliance". I have long been talking, as a diversity and inclusion consultant, about how diverse voices in the room will lead to greater creativity. If we have different perspectives, we are more likely to create different outputs. It makes sense to me that this would extend to neurodiversity. I speak to Wayne Deakin, a creative with a 'diverse mind' who agrees to talk at the event. He tells me, "I want to paint a positive light on it and illustrate that fear and uncertainty are the only barriers in my opinion. I haven't spoken about it up until now because I thought it might be career limiting. But now I've proven you can have a successful career I want to speak out to support others. Genuinely, more people should start seeing this as their superpowers."

The thing that is definitely true, is that we haven't encouraged people with autism to show up as themselves. We haven't even encouraged them to be open about their diagnoses. When working with women in the workplace, I have always walked a fine line between encouraging them to show up as themselves – many of them bring a unique feminine energy to their leadership, which I believe is transformational – and also being pragmatic about the workplace in which they are going to have to succeed. While I champion authenticity above all, someone like Sheryl Sandberg

75   https://auticon.co.uk/autism/

in *Lean In*[76] is, to my mind, more focused on women adapting to the workplace culture that currently exists so as to be successful there. I realise we are walking the same line when talking about neurodiversity.

We want those with diverse minds to be able to show up as themselves to work – the essence of inclusion. However, at the moment, we do not have workplace cultures that facilitate that to happen. From the start, autism interventions seem, to me, to be focused on asking the child with autism to adapt to fit the world that the majority lives in. In the future, it is not the person with autism that needs 'fixing'. It is the workplace culture. We simply have to welcome, accommodate and support a wider range of 'normal', and only then will we benefit from the extraordinary difference these diverse minds can bring.

The challenge of constantly having to adapt and mould yourself to fit an environment has been clear to me from my coaching for years. So many women have lost sight of who they are in the workplace as they attempt to emulate the masculine variety of leadership that tends to be successful in large corporates. It leads to mental health problems, in my opinion. And it is certainly clear to me that those with autism are extraordinarily more likely to struggle with their mental health. Shockingly, a charity called Autistica has found a link between autism and suicide in 10% of the cases[77]. This was debated in November 2017 in an extremely poorly attended MPs debate in the Commons.

Which brings me back to my own resilience. In the midst of my grief, I may well have wished that my son wasn't affected by autism. That thought feels foreign to me now. The history of the medical profession is of wanting to 'fix' or 'change' those

76   Sandberg, Sheryl (2013) *Lean In: Women, Work, and the Will to Lead*

77   http://researchbriefings.parliament.uk/ResearchBriefing/Summary/CDP-2017-0245#fullreport

with autism. It is only by investing a lot of time in taking a good look around when I was in this dark place, that I have realised that people like Leo do not need fixing. They need a world where people accept them for who they are. They need us to stop using phrases like 'risk of autism' in scientific periodicals[78]. What must seeing that do to their sense of self? We need to stop being so scared by difference, lose the stigma and appreciate the gifts.

When we're talking about resilience, I now think we need people who will wade into their discomfort and take a good look around there. Our culture has framed resilience as a way of 'beating' the pain and I'm beginning to believe it to be hugely unhelpful. Through this new lens, the people I see classified as 'resilient' are the ones that may well be hiding from and numbing their pain. I think we need to share our stories of pain – not least because it gives others the permission to feel their own. Too often we might call someone who is visibly demonstrating their pain as 'not resilient enough' and it's again hugely unhelpful. It's a sign of our inability to be with emotion, not a sign of weakness. Staring into our pain and allowing ourselves to feel it is an act of courage.

Equally, it doesn't all have to be about the hard stuff. Thanks to Brené Brown speaking at Courage Camp, I was reminded that equally we need to find the moments of joy within our lives when it's hard. I believe painful feelings are temporary and will weaken over time, as long as we don't try to resist or avoid them. Much of our pain is actually caused by the head telling us that we should be doing better. I've done it to myself this month – calling myself out for still being in struggle a year on. I noticed that the resistance to the struggle was what was creating the pain, not the original struggle itself. The only way is to go through it.

78   https://spectrumnews.org/news/link-parental-age-autism-explained/

And that takes as long as it takes. Maybe resilience isn't about bouncing back, but is instead about wading through.

Writing is a way to wade through. Sitting with my laptop over the past year and exploring my inner world has been a hugely useful tool to bring honesty and clarity to what is really going on for me. In what felt like a full circle, James Pennebaker (an American social psychologist and professor at the University of Texas at Austin) gave the keynote speech at this second Courage Camp explaining how his research has shown that writing increases well-being. In *Writing to Heal*[79] he outlines the landmark research he undertook in the 1980s involving free- or flow-writing, and also offers guided writing prompts. In short, he found that expressive writing is related to wellness. Writing for twenty minutes a day about emotional upheaval can generate positive health benefits – research that has been replicated hundreds of times with positive outcomes.

We may feel saddened in the time immediately after writing, however these feelings generally go away completely in an hour or two. I really had no idea about this research when I started writing – I just knew I had hundreds of thoughts swirling around my mind that were creating anxiety for me. Once I had them out on the page, it seemed to mean that I could stop thinking about them for a while. Writing has cleared my mind – it has been a way to focus briefly on what is happening for me and my feelings related to it, and to then continue with my day. Pennebaker certainly wouldn't be advising everyone to write a book. His research had people free-writing (i.e. writing as it flows out of your brain, without paying attention to structure, grammar or spelling), without the intention of anybody else ever reading it.

The exploration of challenging feelings such as grief and shame has played a critical role for me in moving through them

---

79   Pennebaker, James (2004) *Writing To Heal: A Guided Journey for Recovering from Trauma and Emotional Upheaval*

and reaching acceptance of my son's diagnosis. I have come through the other side of this year with some views that differ from those of health professionals and as a fierce critic of the way in which parents are left stranded after a diagnosis. I see how disability is created largely by a culture which has created a 'normal' way of being. I want my son to live in a world where he can be who he is and be accepted and loved because of all that he is. For all of our children, I want there to be the widest possible range of normal. My son is not broken. And neither am I.

Ways to cultivate resilience when your life is diverted.

1   Stop using resilience as a stick with which to beat yourself. Your life course has been changed. This will take a while to adapt to, there is no exact road map and it will take as long as it takes. While I encourage taking time to feel the difficult emotions, do watch out for thoughts that may make your pain more pronounced, such as when you tell yourself you *should* be feeling better by now.

2   Find moments of joy and let yourself feel them. A work in progress for me, this one. While ending up on a different life path to the one you had planned, and bringing up a child with autism, can be downright difficult and depleting, that does not mean that you are not allowed to experience joy. The essay 'Welcome to Beirut' reminds us that "the smallest improvement will look like a huge leap to you. You will marvel at typical development and realize how amazing it is. You will know sorrow like few others and yet you will know joy above joy". You could also give yourself permission to do joyful things solely for yourself.

3   Try writing. Research has consistently shown that writing for twenty minutes a day about your difficulties has positive health benefits. Hell, you may even end up helping others by telling your story too.

Acknowledgments

Thank you to my teachers, especially Brené Brown and Kristin Neff. Thank you to Leo's Year One teachers for creating trust in the classroom for Leo – Mrs Korbay, Ms Veitch, Miss Anna and Ms Lenaerts. Thank you to my communities, in particular the Gatehouse School "Supporting each other" parents group, the Daring Europe and Africa community and the wider Daring Way™ community. Thank you to the early readers – Harriet, Rachael, Ali and Sandy. Thank you to my angels – Jen and Bo, you really made a difference to me when times were tough. Thank you to Leo's Godparents, Justin, Lex and Paul, for always seeing Leo as Leo. Thank you to my family – Nana Cherry for all of your practical support, Steve for being alongside me no matter what and Finn for innately understanding what Leo needs whilst being aware of your own needs. Also for always brightening up the room. And Leo – thank you for teaching me so much and for being my boy wonder.

Praise for Diverted

This book is a gift to anyone living with a loved one who has autism. The insight, vulnerability, and courage in the author's writing is an invitation to sit along side her and feel our way through this journey together.

Sandy Mitsch, Daring Way™ senior faculty

Beautifully written and easy to read.

Ali Hanan, founder and CEO Creative Equals

Broke my heart and then mended it again. I loved this book. Honest, vulnerable and insightful, a true look at modern family life. Brave and heartwarming, I couldn't put it down.

Harriet Minter, journalist and broadcaster

Rox had me at 'Understanding what other parents are going through is invaluable at a time when you feel so alone; that it is only you that is going through such difficulty.' Each time the school called talking about behaviours, and 'refusal to follow instruction' reinforced the feeling of being alone, that I was the only one dealing with all this – school, assessment centres, the struggle to gets needs recognised and the ongoing struggle to have these needs met. Of course now I know I'm not but like Roxanne, I was pulling out every tool in the coaching box to try and support myself through this so reading Rox's book was a relief – at the time we were pre-diagnosis but just the recognition of emotions – guilt, shame, attempting to be my version of what I thought resilience was… Rox's words gave me permission to be kinder to myself, and importantly, reminded me that even the experts don't have all the answers – which was more reassuring than I first thought as it gave me back my trust in my intuition that I do *know* my child and fired me up to do right by him, while also taking care of me. It's also an excellent education on neurodiversity and the wide range of research and approaches, with plenty of information for further research. Part parental memoir, part self-help (honest, vulnerable and yet empowering), I look forward to hearing more from Rox on this subject.

Rachael Blair, poet and copywriter